A
PRISONER
AND YET ...

CORRIE TEN BOOM

A
PRISONER
AND YET ...

PUBLICATIONS
Fort Washington, PA 19034

A Prisoner and Yet . . .
Published by CLC Publications

U.S.A.
P.O. Box 1449, Fort Washington, PA 19034

UNITED KINGDOM
CLC International (UK)
Unit 5, Glendale Avenue, Sandycroft, Flintshire, CH5 2QP

Printed in the United States of America

ISBN (paperback): 978-0-87508-019-2
ISBN (e-book): 978-1-936143-71-9

Faith's Compassion
... and Strength

Throughout her months in Nazi concentration camps, Corrie ten Boom saw sickness, suffering, torture and mass murder. She was among the human flotsam herded into foul boxcars enroute to new terror.

She was one of the "lucky" ones who served the Reich through slave labor; one of the "privileged" who slept two to a 27 1/2-inch lice-infested cot; who lived to see stealing, treachery and worse among the prisoners—but also witnessed sacrifice . . . and love.

A Prisoner and Yet . . . is her strong and poignant memoir of an historic tragedy, and of the unwavering faith that brought her strength—and survival—when she needed it most.

Contents

Casper ten Boom (father of the author) and Elizabeth (sister). Both gave their lives in prison.

The author in the center, with her father and sister.

Prelude

Daddy, do you know that you haven't tucked me in?"
What a weight of reproach there can be in the voice of a child!

"Yes, dear, I'm coming."

The doctor, with whom I was conversing, excused himself. We both understood that being tucked in was of much greater importance than any economic problems we might be discussing. He went upstairs, and I heard the slight sounds of a minute's romping, the chatter of two child-voices, and then the footsteps of the doctor as he returned down the stairs. We went on with our conversation, but my mind was no longer really on the subject.

The doctor and his wife were Jews.

The Gestapo might arrive at any moment to snatch those children from their beds and drag them off to some camp for a sudden or lingering death! Would the father be taken away from his family, and the mother mourn for her children in far-away Poland?

"Daddy, do you know that you haven't tucked me in?"

A resolution took form in my heart:

I shall help the Jews wherever I can!

Two members of God's ancient people for whom the author's father gave his life, willingly.

Listening to the forbidden radio in the ten Boom home.

Introduction

How can I write a foreword to a book like this? I am taken out of my depth, both in the horrors endured and in the tender compassion of Christ which shines through all the scenes. Man is a dreadful, demonic being in the deeps of his fallen nature; not by any means only the terrible fellow-humans we meet with in these pages, but all humanity, did we but really see ourselves as God knows us to be, shorn of the moral influences and civilizing refinements which sustain us. I have often wondered at the drastic descriptions of the sheer wickedness, malice and degradation of man, both in heart and act, so constantly presented to us as the true facts of our natures in the Scriptures. My knowledge of myself, or the little I really know of myself but for the grace of God, bears these out; but I have had a job to believe this is really so of all my neighbors without that same grace. But it is, and this record drives it home to me with appalling force. These were not primitive savages, or so-called "heathen," but members of a so-called "Christian" nation. Let us beware and learn, for all are alike in their basic nature, yes, each of us readers; and prophecies such as the book of Revelation give us fair warning of the horrible harvest of evil and suffering, proceeding out of the evil heart of Satan and man, which is the destiny of this world, till its rightful King returns in person. Let us be sure that we have personally found the only change of our nature possible through the personal acceptance of the only Savior.

That transforming miracle is what radiates through this otherwise terrible book. We see, not Satan triumphant, nor hardened and wicked men and women, but the compassionate, conquering Christ. How marvelous to see the rest, the sweetness, the joy He actually gives, and gives continually, to one in months of solitary confinement, and equally in months of crowded conditions with never one hour alone, in filth, vermin, stench, starvation, cold, rough toil, amid curses, the whip, and hours and hours of weansome standing and shivering on parades. And more wonderful still, how He lifts the one, in whom He lives, above herself, and immerses her in the dreadful sufferings of those around her: an angel in hell, but no, much more than an angel, the Christ of the Cross living again His own beautiful life of pity and power among the tormented.

None could really write these things but one who had experienced them, for this is no highly-polished reporter's story. Christ-filled Christians are still humans; they suffer and question and shrink, even as they follow; out of weakness they are made strong; and in Corrie ten Boom again we hear the human cry of the Great Sufferer in His darkest hour, "If it be possible let this cup pass from me"; but also those words of triumph which took Him through His cross, "Nevertheless, not as I will, but as thou wilt" (Matt. 26:39).

Yes, this is a book of triumph through Christ, a triumph transmitted to many another in those awful places of torment; and it cannot but put faith and hope into the heart of any reader who, knowing himself, is tempted to wonder if he too can endure his appointed cross. He too will say to himself, "Yes, I can, by Corrie's Christ."

N.P. Grubb
London

1

The House in the Barteljorisstraat

Life in the Underground

The music of one of Tartini's sonatas filled the drawing room of our home in the Barteljorisstraat. All around were people in listening attitudes, concentrating on the music. The violinist was a young lawyer who had been forced underground, and was now a guest in our home because he had become depressed in his previous environment.

For our home, it was often said, "was the gayest underground address in all the Netherlands." And, indeed, there was harmony and happiness here, though not unmixed with care, or undisturbed by threats of grave danger.

Eusie was to sing for us next. There was a moment of absolute silence as the last tender note of the violin sonata died away. But the stillness was suddenly broken by the distant rumble of antiaircraft guns and the joyless singing of German soldiers in the street.

Then Eusie stood at the piano. He was a cantor and had a beautiful voice. Passionately he sang his Jewish song, pouring out the longing, the grief, and the indignation of his race. He was, for the moment, an interpreter of the age-old anguish of Israel.

But he was singing too loudly, and I had to warn him "Eusie, they will hear you out in the street; and everyone will know there is a Jew in the house! You must sing more softly or stop singing altogether."

I was sorry to put an end to it all; but Eusie was like an overgrown boy. He could not realize how completely Jewish he was in person and manner, nor understand that that very fact meant danger to himself and to those about him.

The atmosphere had suddenly become strained. When, oh when, would this menace pass and we again be permitted to enjoy freely the good things of life?

I went to the piano and started playing, and a quartette took up the melody:

> *"Come now with song of melody sweet,*
> *Rejoicing with stringed instrument."*

The happy ten Boom family during the war. The music of Tartini's sonatas fills the drawing room.

There were both trained and untrained voices among the singers, but their voices blended in perfect harmony. We were once more completely engrossed in our music, when I was called away.

Downstairs in the hall, like frightened animals escaping the chase, stood a Jewish couple, pleading for shelter. I took them into the dining room and gave them some hot coffee. The man's hands were trembling so that he could hardly hold the cup, and he spilled the coffee. His teeth were chattering; and he began a confused tale of all the wealth they had had to leave behind: a beautiful leather traveling-bag, linens, provisions, and magnificent Oriental rugs.

They had been safely under cover. But that night a warning had come: they had been betrayed—and the S.D.[1] were already on the way to seize them.

"Of course you are welcome to stay here for the night, and then we shall see. We'll take care of you. Try not to be frightened, for everything will come out all right."

I left them downstairs with Father, who knew so well how to comfort people. And he loved the Jews. Our family had always loved Jehovah's covenant people, even in previous generations.

Upstairs, our refugee guests and I talked things over. Hans, the student, could sleep in the "Angelcrib," as we called our hidden closet behind a blind wall. There was a grilled vent in it to admit fresh air, and we could leave the sliding door open. Then the Jewish woman could have Hans' little room, and her husband would sleep with the boys.

But nine refugees were too many for our small house, so Peter went out at once to look for another underground address. When he returned at almost ten he had still found nothing. The first house was filled; in the second were children, who could not be depended upon to keep quiet about Jewish guests. Another had Dutch Nazi neighbors. And so, as we prayed that evening, there were two more burdens to cast upon the Lord.

Early the next morning the stream of co-workers in the underground began to pour in. I asked each one, "Do you know of a place for a Jewish couple?" Fred knew of an opening for the day after tomorrow, and I hurried off to tell Tante Mien,[2] which was the new name we had given to our latest arrival. She was in the kitchen, peeling potatoes with Eusie and the other boys. Hank, the violinist, was telling jokes, and they were having a jolly time. How different from the first days that Hank had been with us! Then he would sit for hours, silently staring into space. Later he revealed himself to be a young fellow who, though quiet, was also full of fun, and capable of arousing the gales of laughter I now heard in the kitchen. Oom Jan, the second new guest, was sitting beside Father smoking his pipe. When I informed them there would be a place for them in a day or two, both he and his wife begged to be allowed to stay with us here. But that was impossible. Leaving it to my sister Betsie (she was seven years older than I) to convince them, I hurried upstairs, where many people were waiting for my attention.

"Do you have a place for a Jewish child?"

"How do I procure a green Ausweiss?"[3]

One boy had come all the way from Limburg. With other boys and girls he worked in an organization which cared for hundreds of Jewish children. One of the girls had with her eight psychopathic cases, boys and girls of all ages. The problem of their care seemed to have reached an impasse.

"Is there some psychiatrist you can consult? Good. Ask him to make up a report on them, and I shall see that they are placed in the proper institutions."

What a busy day! The problems piled up. A Jewish woman was about to give birth; I, myself, would have to find time to confer with the hospital authorities. Somewhere, a child had contracted diphtheria. A man had died and I had to arrange for a clandestine burial.

That day I dispatched couriers to Limburg, Friesland and Enschede. My room resembled a beehive; it was, indeed, a sort of clearing house for supply and demand. I met the needs of one with help provided by another.

"You know of a place for a child? Fine! Make arrangements with Marie over there; she has an emergency case. She has also asked for Ausweissen. Dick, you know what to do about that."

"Twenty more ration cards? Right, you shall have them. Jim, fetch twenty-five cards out of the stair cubbyhole. Mies will soon be here for five more." (The stair cubbyhole was one of our hidden storage places inside the top step of the staircase. No one would ever suspect that there was a cupboard there.)

In a small shed on the public tennis courts a man was lying, seriously ill. He had been there when his host was arrested. He himself barely escaped. That evening people would be playing on the courts, and the man had to be removed before six. The courts were beyond Santpoort.

"All right, boys, let's get busy. Who will arrange for transportation? Who for an address?"

My fine, capable boys jumped up and talked things over. In a few minutes there was silence, as each one of them slipped out on his errand.

What attractive young people they were! Such fresh, strong faces! There were some resolute characters among these boys and girls. They were serious for their age, and were doing independent, responsible work. Human lives depended on their faithfulness and no less on their ability to maintain silence.

They felt at home with me. If they were too busy to go home, which was not infrequent; they ate and slept in the Beje. "Beje" was the pseudonym for Barteljorisstraat. Occasionally there was time for a chat about their own difficulties and troubles; and then they would confide in me the secrets which were far more characteristic of their age than the problems with which they were occupied throughout most of the day.

Not until ten o'clock that evening did I find time to get my records into shape. I had missed the class in Italian. Mary, our eldest refugee, who formerly conducted a travel bureau in Italy, was teaching it. Eusie taught Hebrew; Hans, Astronomy. Jim felt he could not compete with all these scholars. He could, however, give an evening's program of magic. His tricks were a bit obvious, but they provided us with a diversion and created a cheerful atmosphere. Everyone attended the class in Italian. Even Father came with his notebook. His eighty-four years did not keep him from broadening his knowledge of languages, for language study was one of his hobbies.

It was great fun to have so many people in the house!

We sat at the oval table in the dining room with our chairs a bit aslant, for that was the only way we could all get around it. We sat so close together that the cat (deservedly and elaborately named Maher Shalal Hashbaz, which means "hastening to the spoil, hurrying to the prey") had devised a little game of walking about from one shoulder to another until he came to rest on Grandfather's.

Our spirits were a bit uproarious that day. How different was our house from what it appeared to be to the outside world—the home of three more or less old people!

Suddenly, a ladder was placed against the window, and the faces about the table tightened, especially those of our latest guests. They turned pale with fright. Fortunately it was only the window cleaner, come to wash the windows. What a relief! But still . . . suppose the man should be a traitor? How could we explain the presence of so many people in our house? Eusie had an idea: "We'll pretend it's Aunt Betsie's birthday, and sing the traditional song, 'Happy birthday to you!'"

Deep basses, altos, and sopranos, all tried to sing along. But laughter kept us from finishing the "beautiful" song.

"Eusie, go and sit with your back to the window."

"That will do no good," said Hans, "even his neck is Semitic."

"Can this always go on this way?" I wondered. I had a small Bible tucked away in my clothes, and a pencil hidden in my hair. Some day, I felt certain, things would go wrong.

The number of our co-workers increased by the day. We had already sheltered more than eighty refugees in the Beje for varying periods of time, though our guests had never been fewer than seven or more than twelve in number at one time. One small nucleus always remained. Eusie, Mary, and later, Martha, were Jews. Then there were Peter and Hans, who were students, and Leonard, a teacher. The latter were refugees who worked with the underground. And all of them helped with the household tasks. The house was becoming a bit untidy, for there was no really expert help to be had; but we did the best we could. The most important thing, in any case, was that people should be rescued, and next that they should have a happy home. And repeated scoldings about tidiness did not fit into that picture. Things that were formerly so important were now relegated to the background.

Safety measures were tremendously important. Consequently we practiced safety drills. After everyone had gone to bed, I would press one of the alarm bells that had been installed throughout the house. With a stop watch in hand I would stand by, while everyone disappeared into my closet. Under the bottom shelf was a sliding door, behind which was the secret space where approximately eight people could stand. On the floor of this hiding place was a mattress, a supply of Victoria water,[4] and some Sanovit.[5] Every night before retiring all of our guests-in-transit would bring their outer and underclothing into the Angelcrib. It was a comic sight. Eusie's braces always trailed along after him as he carried in his clothes. One of the boys would go inside and hang all the clothing on a hallstand. In our drills, however, they themselves would also disappear. They ducked down and vanished under the shelf; the last I saw of them was their legs. Then they would place boxes and laundry on the floor of the closet and shove down the sliding door.

Seventy seconds it took them. I made the rounds of the rooms. They looked uninhabited, the mattresses turned over, the blankets folded underneath. The sheets were taken along into hiding. Eusie had left some cigar ashes, and Hans a collar stud. From the Angelcrib I could hear Eusie's very Jewish voice, "Mary, you're blowing on my neck!" I called them out, and everyone sat on the floor in front of my bed as we cheerfully talked over the drill. Eusie's ashes, the collar stud and the noisy remark were all discussed.

It was a pity that we had to have these drills. We all felt keenly the tragic necessity of them, and so I used to ease the situation by treating the group to cream puffs. They all knew that this was the customary conclusion to our drills, and Eusie would often say, "Aren't we going to have an alarm tonight? I'm hungry for cream puffs."

Enemy Raid

On February 28, 1944, came the actual alarm. I was lying abed with influenza and had a vaporizer burning to relieve my congested bronchia. Past the bed raced four Jewish refugees, followed into the hiding place by two underground workers, who were also in great danger because they were carrying incriminating papers on their persons. I threw my briefcase of records in after them, placed the boxes in front of the opening, and closed the closet door. I was just back in my bed when I heard heavy footsteps on the stairs. A surly-looking man entered my room.

"Who are you? Give me your identification card."

Out of a small bag I drew my identification card. A packet of bank notes came out with it. The man seized it greedily and thrust it into his pocket, looked at my identification card and said, "Get up at once; you're my prisoner."

As I dressed I could hear other men walking through the house, and the sound of hammer blows against a door.

"Where is your secret room?" demanded the man.

"I won't tell you."

"Oh, yes you will. But, of course, that is where your Jews are hidden. Never mind; I'll have the house watched until they've turned into mummies." A fiendish smile played about his cruel mouth.

Coming downstairs, I found the dining room filled with people. My brother had just conducted a Bible study group which had been well attended. And now everyone who crossed our threshold was arrested. The Beje had become a Gestapo trap. The captain who was in charge of the raid, a man with a pale, cruel face, ordered me to accompany him to my shop.

"Take off your glasses," he snarled.

Then began my "interrogation." After every question he gave me a slap in the face. I grew dizzy after the first blow. For a minute I had a severe pain which did, however, subside fairly soon. But as he continued slapping me I began to fear that I would not be able to endure it.

"Lord Jesus, protect me!" I cried aloud.

A horrible expression crept over his cruel face. He hissed at me, "If you mention that name once more I shall kill you." But he stopped beating me.

Then Betsie was brought in and I was sent back to the dining room. But I was not given a chance to pick up my glasses and had to do without them for weeks. When Betsie returned, my other sister asked, "Were you beaten?"

"Yes," said Betsie, "and I do so pity the man who beat me."

When the captain had continued striking her also she called out, "O Savior, Savior!" He shouted at her, "Silence! Don't use that name!" But again he stopped, abruptly.

The entire house was searched. A closet in the dining room, which we had not considered safe as a hiding place for people but where we had hidden many valuables, was discovered. Out of it came a large number of silver "rijksdaalders"[6] we had saved. They were thrown on the table and then vanished into the captain's pouch. Boxes of watches belonging to Jews, and other knick-knacks, followed.

Meanwhile, all of those who had fallen into the Nazi trap were sitting or standing along the walls. No one said a word, and there was something ominous about the silence.

My father was very calm as he sat in his chair beside the fire. I started to go to him, but one of the Gestapo turned my chair about and made me sit facing the wall. I no longer had anything to say in my own home. Was there anger in my heart because of this humiliating treatment? No, only concern for all the people about me. "Oh, dear," I thought, "there comes Missionary Lass-chuit; he too will fall into the trap and be arrested."

An old woman was babbling unsuspectingly to one of the Gestapo in the hall. "Mijnheer. I have come to report that Uncle Herman has been seized. The folk here had better look out, too. Will you tell them for me that they must be careful?"

"Yes, indeed," replied the Gestapo man with feline sweetness, "whom, for instance, should I warn?"

"Oh, I don't know; just all those people who come to this house."

Then the telephone rang. I had been a bit proud of having kept that telephone a secret, and of having been able to help many people make clandestine telephone connections by my intervention. But now I heard it with fear and dismay. I was compelled to take the calls with one of the Gestapo men beside me, listening in. I tried as much as possible to indicate by my voice that something was very wrong here.

Over and over I heard the same message, "Do you know that Uncle Herman has been apprehended? Do be careful! You, too, are in danger."

If only I dared to shout into the phone, "Yes, I know; we also have been arrested and one of the Gestapo men is standing here beside me, listening to our conversation." But I did not dare. I had respect for the hand of that human beast in my hall.

Then one of the men tried to put in a call, but got no response. The clandestine connection was broken. They had understood my unspoken thought.

The captain was furious. "How does it happen that the connection is broken? Do you have a secret number?"

Innocently, I answered, "I know nothing about it; I don't understand what has happened." But, secretly, I was greatly relieved. There would be no more telephone calls. People knew our misfortune.

And now I was, after all, sitting beside Father and trying to stir the fire. Betsie was serving bread. I could scarcely get it down, but observed that our servant accepted it hungrily. Poor man, how wretched for him to have been arrested also! His wife and children will be so distressed.

As my glance met Betsie's she pointed to our lovely new fireplace. There, against the tiles, hung a simple pokerwork plaque which read: "Jesus is Victor." Father followed the direction of my glance and said aloud, "Yes, indeed, that is absolutely true."

There seemed to be a visible relaxation in the faces of those around us, now that someone had broken the silence. Or was it, perhaps, because they, too, had read the text?

"It looks now," I mused, "as if the Gestapo were the conquerors. But they are not. I do not understand it all, but believing is not the same as understanding."

Suddenly one of the Gestapo said to Father, "I see a Bible over there. Tell me, what does it say about the government?"

And Father answered, "Fear God; honor the queen."

"That is not true; the Bible doesn't say that."

"No, it says 'Fear God and honor the king,' but in our case that is the queen."

The cat jumped up on my lap and rubbed her soft fur against me. It touched me so. What would become of her pretty soon, after the house was empty?

I was almost thankful when we started out for the police station in the Smedestraat. Father leaned heavily on my arm. Passing the Frisian clock in the hall he suggested that I pull up the weights. Didn't he realize that tomorrow he would no longer be here in this house with his beloved clock?

During all this time our six refugees and co-workers were safely hidden in our secret chamber. The Gestapo knew they were there but could not locate the room. Our house was so old and so curiously constructed that no one could see that in one room there were two stone walls, between which there was space enough for eight persons.

A guard of two policemen was left to watch the house. After two and a half days, policemen who were sympathetic to the underground were on duty. They had been informed of the plight of the poor prisoners by our co-workers, and as soon as it was safe, released them. How thankful they were to escape from their cramped quarters! Not until dark did they dare to venture out into the street. Eusie was so happy to be outside that he raised his arms in the middle of the street and chanted a Jewish prayer. Would the boy never be sensible?

At the police station a large mattress was placed on the floor for our sleeping accommodation. I counted thirty-five prisoners. All of Father's children, three daughters, one son, and one grandson, shared the mattress with him.

"I once saw this in a dream," said Betsie. "I didn't understand what it meant, but I saw Father and all of his children and many others lying on a mattress."

Before we lay down Father gathered us all about him. At his request my brother read Psalm 91, and then Father prayed. How often in the past I had heard my father praying! And his voice, even now, was as calm and tranquil as ever before. This was the last time that he was to pray with us, although I did not realize it then.

A policeman was sitting in the room on guard. He was friendly, and as he looked at Father I could see an expression of sadness come into his eyes.

"He is very likely the oldest prisoner you have ever had to guard, isn't he?" I asked.

"Things are bad enough," he grumbled, in reply.

Since we had been left almost entirely to ourselves, we had an excellent opportunity to plan together, quietly, what answers we should give in case we were brought to trial. How should we explain all of those people coming to our house?

But we were warned to be on our guard, and just in time! A certain watchmaker, a colleague of my father, had ostensibly been arrested with us. He was really a *provocateur*.[7] As we talked together he came and stood behind us.

Leaving Haarlem

The day that followed upon that sleepless night was long and tedious. We could not expect pleasant events, yet we longed for something to happen. "Once we are in our prison cells," we told one another, "we shall be able to rest."

At noon a large bus stopped at the station. As we stepped into it we saw many fellow citizens standing about. Everyone was quiet. Haarlem loved my father. "Haarlem's Grand Old Man" was its favorite name for him. And now his friends and neighbors were standing in the street, most of them with tears in their eyes.

The Grote Markt looked so beautiful; the sun was shining down on the Grote Kerk. It was a radiant February day, and one could already feel something of spring in the air. Haarlem's last greeting was a bright and sunny one. When would I see it again?

"Just think, Father, when we next see Haarlem, it will be free."

"No," said Betsie, "you will see it before then."

I had my arm around my father, and he leaned heavily against me. He was very weak, and we spoke only about heaven.

"The best is yet to come" had always been one of Father's favorite expressions.

"Whatever comes to pass, heaven awaits us," we reminded him.

"That is certainly true," said Father.

He was neither restless nor sad. It occurred to me that he did not quite realize where he was going.

· · · · ·

In my heart was a great sense of peace. I had long expected this catastrophe. Now the blow had fallen. I accepted it as the close of an exciting chapter of my life.

In my mind I kept telling myself, "Don't ever feel sorry for yourself."

2

In Prison at Scheveningen

Father's Last Days

In Scheveningen we were brought to the Bureau of the Gestapo. My sister said to the officers, "My father is so ill and weak he will not be able to take that high step into the auto."

"Don't worry, Mevrouw,"[8] was the answer, "we shall carry him." And they did carry him carefully. In the car Father leaned back, his mouth fell open, and then it occurred to me for the first time that he might never return.

As Father was carried into the Bureau a German said, "You might as well let that man die at home."

"What!" yelled the captain. "That man is the worst of them all. He talks about nothing but Jesus and the queen."

It was still quite a distance from the Bureau to the prison, and we were shoved into a patrol car. It reminded me of the tumbrils in the stories of the French Revolution. It was a horrible vehicle, without springs, and jolted continually. Father lay in my arms. Even one of the officers helped to support him to ease the worst jolts.

And then the gate of the great prison closed behind us.

"*Alle nasen gegen mauer!*" (Every nose to the wall!) And there

ᴀ facing the wall. Father was allowed to sit on a chair. I
ᴅ a kiss on his forehead, that noble forehead!

The Lord be with you," I whispered.

"And with you," was his reply.

I turned and looked back once more. It was my last glimpse
of Father on earth. He was to survive his arrest by only ten days.
In the cell he was reported to have been very courageous, saying to
his cellmates: "If I am released tomorrow I shall go on the day after
tomorrow giving aid to the Jews, and shelter and help to all who
need it." Long afterwards I learned that during his last days his mind
was confused. He was brought to a hospital, where he died in the
corridor. They buried him in a pauper's grave. The date was March
9, 1944. When he died his children and youngest grandson were in
the same prison. What little effort it would have required to bring
us to him. But we were not allowed even to know that he had died.

A nephew at home read the death notice in the paper, on the
very day that two of Father's grandchildren had gone to the Hague
to pick up whatever information they could about their grandfather's
condition. They were sent from pillar to post and were finally told
in some office, "Oh, your grandfather was buried yesterday."

On the label of a package sent to Betsie a niece wrote: "Do not
grieve about Grandfather. He has gone where no one can do him
any more harm and where he always longed so much to go. 'The
best is yet to come' was his motto, and now the 'best' has come
for him. Keep courage, Auntie; it is the best way."

People had often warned Father, "If you persist in harbor-
ing so many Jews you will eventually end in prison, and in your
delicate condition you could never survive that."

And Father would answer, "If that should come to pass I shall
consider it an honor to give my life for God's ancient people."

That honor had now been bestowed upon him. Father had
died in prison, a martyr's death.

When Betsie heard about it she wrote home: "Anyone . . . who
lived so close to the Savior, to whom spiritual things were so real,

Casper ten Boom, 84 years of age, father of the author.

and who had in such a glorious measure the gift of prayer, such a person has all the prerequisites for martyrdom. I have always thought, 'He will never die in his bed.'"

God had not permitted the reins of government to slip from His fingers.

In My Cell

I was thrust into a cell. Lying on the floor were four persons, among whom were a young baroness and an Austrian charwoman from the Wehrmacht![9] They welcomed me kindly.

"I'm sorry that I must share your very limited space," I said politely. They showed me a wooden cot against the wall and gave me some bread and water. I was literally famished. After eating, I stretched out on the hard, uneven ·mattress and in a very short time fell asleep.

In the morning I was awakened by the opening of the sliding bolt of the cell door. It sounded as if someone were giving the door a vigorous kick. The lights went on, harsh, glaring lights, unsoftened by shades of any sort.

Now I could quietly get acquainted with my cellmates. They were friendly and a bit surprised that I had not cried when brought in. I tried to orient myself in each of their lives. One of them, a woman from Amsterdam's working class, had already been there for two years. She had had much experience of prison life, and showed me how to talk through a secret aperture with the tailor in the next cell. She was informed on all that went on, was always on the alert for news, and had a sharpened sense of hearing.

"There comes Mopje," she would say. "She is bringing the socks for cell 730."

"Oh, dear, someone in cell 742 has to go for a hearing."

"I hear unfamiliar footsteps among the prisoners who work in the corridor; do you suppose there is a new one among them?"

Her chatter was diverting but also disturbing.

When the cell door was opened for the removal of the *kubel*[10]and dirty water, the young baroness would stand at the door as long as possible to get a bit of fresh air. I thought, "We are deprived of the simplest requirements for health: air, exercise and cleanliness." The mattresses were so dirty that they sent showers of dust over everything when we piled them up for the day. The dust made my cough worse and reminded me that I was still sick. After the cell had been mopped, things became quiet around us and a boredom settled down upon us which I later learned to fear.

Frau Mikes, the Austrian woman, sat quietly weeping. She was so concerned about her canary. "The poor creature will surely die; no one will take care of him. I was picked up just as I was and had no time to ask anyone."

That reminded me of our cat. The last minute we were at home she jumped up into my lap, purring and rubbing her head against me. Just thinking about it made me feel weak. I could understand the grief of the poor woman and spoke softly to her and tried to comfort her. Presently she was telling me the pathetic story of her life. She had been married several times, and each time had been so maltreated by her husband that she had run away. Now she was in love with the flutist in a jazz band.

Strange to have to live in such intimate daily contact with persons of such entirely different backgrounds. But it was an opportunity to enlarge my understanding of people, and I tried to engage all of them in conversation. Each one of them, however, resisted my efforts, and I felt too weary to continue the attempt.

One of the women paced back and forth in the cell the whole day long, like a caged lion, six paces up, six paces back. And she blinked incessantly. How prison does deprive one of the most elementary living conditions! I decided then that if God gave me further opportunities I would engage in some sort of rehabilitation work. I had never before dared to make prison calls, but felt that now I should not hesitate to do so.

To escape boredom I learned to play solitaire. What an innocent game it seemed to be! I thought about Father, who had scruples against all card playing. But he certainly could have nothing against this game.

After a few days, however, I understood the danger of even this apparently innocent game. If the cards came out right our spirits soared, there was hope and confidence that our release would come soon; if not, our spirits sank into the depths.

What a lot of superstition everywhere! Fortune-telling with cards was also a favorite pastime of many prisoners. And they attached such great significance to the outcome.

Two cells away was Mien, a nurse from Haarlem. At great risk we constantly exchanged notes through little holes in the wall.

One morning I awakened with an overwhelming sense of sorrow. I was so distressed about Father. The mattress on which I was lying was very uneven. My hand and arm throbbed with neuritis, and I did not know how to lie. But hardest to bear was my constant worry about Father. He, too, was lying on a mattress as hard as mine, he with his frail body. Would anyone help him? Betsie and I had always surrounded him with the tenderest of care. And now he was in prison. A prayer welled up in my heart: "O Lord, take him home to Thee in heaven. It will be so good for him!"

To Mien I wrote, "I hope that Father will soon be taken home by the Savior. He will enjoy heaven so very much."

It was now the second week of my imprisonment. I had been very ill for three day. Finally, the door opened wide and I was told to get dressed and to put on a coat and hat.

A hat might never be worn in prison, so I understood that I was going outside. I asked the orderly who came to fetch me where we were going.

"To the consultation bureau."

A beautiful car was waiting outside. With two other prisoners, an officer and the orderly, I stepped in.

Then we rode through the Hague. How natural everything looked and yet how unnatural to us. People were walking freely on the streets, street cars were running, there was a bakery wagon, a garbage truck. The sun was shining brightly; the weather was a delight.

In the consultation bureau I asked a nurse if I might wash my hands. She went with me, closed the door behind us and impulsively put her arms around me.

"Can I help you in any way?" she asked.

"Oh, yes, please; do you have a Bible for me? Mine was taken away on entering the prison. And do you have a pencil, a toothbrush, safety pins?" I asked for a number of useful things. Her cordiality did me much good. In appearance she was not an unusually attractive woman, but love radiated from her.

What a contrast to the evil guards in the prison! Does she realize, I wondered, how she has warmed my heart by her friend-liness? I shall always remember this encounter with gratitude.

The doctor concluded that I had pleurisy with effusion. "I hope I am doing you a service in this diagnosis," he said. "They will very likely send you to the hospital."

As I was leaving, the friendly nurse thrust into my pocket many of the articles for which I had asked. She could not get a Bible so quickly, but did find copies of the four Gospels. How happy I was with them!

Solitary Confinement

Two days later, in the evening, I was taken from my cell. "Take everything with you. You are going into solitary confinement." I was not permitted to say a word while collecting my meager possessions. I managed to get my Gospels from underneath the mattress, but failed to save the pencil. A great pity! I said good-bye to my cellmates with a glance. I was sorry to leave them, for I had grown to love them, in spite of the great disparity in our views.

A solitary cell awaited me. I was pushed inside and the door closed after me. I was alone. Everything was empty and gray. In the other cell there had been at least the colors of my cellmates' dresses. Here there was nothing, only an emptiness, a cold gray void. I was chilled to the bone. The wind shrieked, and I felt an icy draft through the cell.

"O Savior, You are with me. Help me; hold me fast and comfort me."

I threw myself down on the mattress, pulled the filthy covers over me, and shut my eyes. The storm howled, and every now and then a gust of wind shook the door so violently it seemed as if someone were beating against it from the outside. To the left and right of me I heard knocking. I did not know then that it was just my neighbors who wanted to talk to me through a slit in the wall under the table. Then water began to gurgle in the pipes of the heating system—a new note in the somber medley of frightening noises.

"Is this a haunted cell into which I have come? O people, people! If only I could see people! Not this! Oh, please, not this loneliness."

"O Savior, take away this anxiety, this desolation."

I felt very ill. My fingers and arm throbbed with pain. I could not find a comfortable position.

"Safe in the arms of Jesus. O my Savior, take me into Your arms and comfort me," I prayed. And peace stole into my heart. The weird noises still surrounded me, but I fell quietly asleep.

Lonely! Alone, I washed my clothing; alone, scrubbed out my cell.

Sick! And there was no one to take care of me. The first few days my bread was thrown to me from the small opening in my cell door, and at times the corridor attendants were allowed to bring my warm meal to my cot. But after three days I had to get up to receive it.

One day a *Sanitäter*[11] called to bring me some medicine. I asked him, "Is my father still living?"

"I don't know, and if I did I would still not be permitted to tell you," was the answer.

A few minutes later the *Wachtmeisterin*[12] stormed in and scolded me angrily. "If you ever dare do such a thing again as ask the *Sanitäter* about another prisoner you will get no medical attention at all as long as you are here."

Temperatures were taken occasionally. A thermometer was then placed in my armpit. But even if I did have a fever it never registered very high in the armpit; and the only result was that when the shutter in my cell door was opened my bread was not thrown to me, but I heard instead: "Get up now, you have no fever."

They taunted me constantly with the fact that I lay abed most of the time. That seemed to be the unpardonable sin. As my temperature was being taken the *Wachtmeisterin* stood by. I took advantage of her presence and tried to talk with her, but she did not even answer me. She seemed to be entirely devoid of human feeling, and altogether hard, hostile, and wicked. These women were so hard and cruel, and they were the only human beings I saw. Why should they always snap and snarl at us? I always greeted them with a pleasant "Good morning," but everything seemed to glance off their impenetrable armor of hate.

I soon grew accustomed to the cell, and when worries threatened to overwhelm me I began to sing. Then I was threatened with *Kalte-kost*[13] or a dark cell if I did not stop singing. *Kalte-kost* meant going without our one warm meal and getting along the whole day with just a bit of bread. However, I did not let them intimidate me, but went on singing again and again. Nevertheless, it was disconcerting when I was wholeheartedly singing a song to have it suddenly cut short by the hoarse, shrieking voice of a furiously angry woman.

When I was permitted to bathe for the first time, the large, somber bathhouse made me feel uneasy. But the shower was wonderful. I had hidden a couple of the Gospels in my clothing, and while waiting for my turn managed to get them into the hands of two of my fellow prisoners. I also hid a couple of pages of a Gospel in a crack I found in one of the stools. They were discovered, however, by the *Wachtmeisterin*, who happened to come in a few minutes later.

Long, long corridors, and many, many doors; and behind each door, imprisoned human beings. Along the middle of the corridor lay a runner of coconut matting. We had to walk alongside of it.

What a change in my life! Formerly, no one would have begrudged me any available luxury. Here I was not allowed to place my feet on coconut matting. And all the people I saw, officers and women guards alike, looked stern, gloomy, and angry. Some of them had cruel faces.

When my cell door closed behind me after my bath I had a pleasant feeling of security. This was *my* cell. Only mine. Away from everything. My table, my cot, my filthy blankets. And the door shut me safely in from the rest of the huge building.

Things That Comforted

Outside the sun was shining. A bird was softly singing a song of spring. Through the twenty-eight rectangles of my window I could see gold-tipped, even clouds. And my fancy took flight. I saw the wide sea, the white-capped waves. I actually heard the murmur of the sea, for the west wind was blowing. I was alone within the close confines of my cell, but outside of my cell was the great prison, and outside of that the great wide world, where birds fly and the sea murmurs. And in that world were people who were thinking about us.

A Red Cross parcel was lying just outside my door. It represented contact with those friendly people who would, perhaps, come very soon to set us free. All the prisoners took courage when the Red Cross parcels arrived on alternate Wednesdays.

The door opened just as I was trying to stand on my trembling legs.

"Come and fetch it yourself; you're walking anyway. I shall not bring it to you." How painful indifference can be!

I unpacked the parcel. It was filled with delicious, tasty things, selected by understanding people who knew what was good for us. Would this, perhaps, be my last parcel? Should we, perhaps, be free in a week or two?

Cookies, a croquette, caramels. But why did I take no delight in these things? There was really no pleasure in nibbling at this or that dainty by myself. It occurred to me to offer some to the *Wachtmeisterin*, but I let the impulse pass.

I knew I would never in the future (was there to be a future?) eat dainties by myself. If ever I had anything good to eat, I would remember cell 384 and invite others to enjoy it with me.

It was dark in my cell.

I talked with my Savior. Never before had fellowship with Him been so close. It was a joy I hoped would continue unchanged. I was a prisoner—and yet . . . how free!

Sick

When one is ill he is over-sensitive; he wants those about him to nurse and care for him the best they can. My arm pained me, at times so severely that I could not sleep, or even lie comfortably. My scantily-filled straw mattress was very uneven. At times it was almost comfortable and I slept well on it; but usually it was thin where it should be thick and vice versa. I often got up four times in a night to turn it. But then the foul dust irritated my throat, and I had to be careful not to cough, for coughing brought up blood. Sometimes I covered the entire mattress with the larger half of my blanket to escape the stench. I put the head end of the mattress against the cold stone wall. The straw pillow always slid off unless I lay very still. That pillow was a filthy thing, warm and smelly from fermenting straw. One of the blankets I pulled over me; the other smelled, so I had to keep it as far as possible from my nose. But the cell was cold. Sometimes in the night I would begin to feel sorry for myself. Then I would list a whole series of complaints to make to the doctor or the *Wachtmeisterin*; but I knew I should never mention them. If only I had a sheet, and another mattress, and blankets, and pillows! The pain in my arm grew more severe. At first I had pills for it, but later on a liquid in a dirty bottle with a black cork. It was supposed to be taken after supper, but sometimes I took a spoonful at noon and again at night. It had a narcotic effect.

I was without the most essential things. I had not been able to bring a toothbrush. One towel was furnished me. I washed the clothes I was wearing in turn, for I had no change of underwear. My table service consisted of a wooden spoon, a wooden knife, and a graniteware mug. A stay out of my corset, ground against the stone wall until it was sharp enough for cutting, served as my knife. Under the folding table hung the dirtiest cloth I had ever seen. I wondered if it was intended to be a dishcloth? I never dared touch it. There was also a wastebasket without a bottom, and a badly leaking washbasin. The seat of the *kubel* stuck so tightly I could scarcely get it off with my weak and trembling hands.

Against the wall, on a nail, hung my fur coat.

Through the rectangular spaces between the window bars the sun was shining in. I had now been in my cell for six weeks and had not once been outside for an airing. The window was high in the wall above the door. Gradually the sunbeams would come low enough for me to reach them. Then I would get up and stand against the wall with my face toward the sun. Following its rays, I would move slowly along the wall until I picked up the last rays while standing on my cot.

There was such a hunger in my heart for sunshine, for freedom, and for home. I had to accept the fact that God had brought me here, but it was very difficult.

Airing

Outside, for the first time in seven weeks! Through the garden gate, a bolted door, I came into the prison garden; and I was there alone. Shrubs, colorful primroses, yellow beach sand, and a wide blue sky. My legs tingled from the unaccustomed exercise, but I walked on and on, along the rectangular path around the center plot. I drank in the colors and the light; and my heart beat fast with emotion.

But then, suddenly, I was seized by an indescribable melancholy. I still saw the colors through my tears. But I felt a loneliness deeper than that of my cell, in and all about me. I no longer saw any beauty in the barren garden, but a sphere of cruelty and death. At the end of the garden was an oblong pit like a newly-dug grave. Half of the shrubs were entirely without leaves because they had been transplanted into dune sands. A high stone wall, with cruel points of glass cemented into the top, surrounded the garden; and to the north stood the tall prison, barren and gray, with row after row of barred windows. Near the south wall I smelled the gruesome stench of burned bones; and I recalled that my nephew, Kik, had once told me, "There are three crematoria at Scheveningen." Beyond the wall, the silence was momentarily shattered by the rattle of a machine gun. Then, again, stillness—deep and ominous. It was two o'clock. Everything about me looked like a city of the dead. The solitude of the garden, for the prisoner in solitary confinement . . .

"And Enoch walked with God" (Gen. 5:24) flashed into my mind. Enoch was not homesick as he walked with God. That thought comforted me and took away the sense of loneliness.

I was no longer alone. God was with me. With Him I could go on; and once more I saw the blue sky, the flowers and shrubs;

and I saw the garden as a part of a beautiful free world, in which I, too, should some day be able to walk about. The earth is, in much the same way, a solitary prison garden, and heaven is the great, free out-of-doors, where fulfillment of joy awaits us, the children of the Light.

Children In Prison

A child was brought into a cell with her aunt, and for half an hour her plaintive little voice cried, "Daddy, I want to go to my Daddy."

The tragedy of this place of misery seemed to be epitomized in that complaint.

How dark that evening was!

The next day the same small voice sang: "The little bell rings; the little bird sings." The sweet child-sound reached out beyond all our misery and directed our thoughts to the last phrase of the song, "The praise and glory of God."

The same cell had previously lodged two still smaller children. Their voices could be heard the whole day long, "Yes, Mummy? Isn't it so, Mummy?"

It made my soul cringe.

Ordinary child-sounds and expressions are so out of place in a prison. But these little ones did not seem to suffer from the cold cell. They remained cheerful. And then one night the *Wachtmeisterin* came to fetch them. They were going on a transport. Where to? No one knows. The next day it was disturbingly quiet around us.

The Hearing

It was oppressively quiet in the prison. The time dragged slowly by. So unlike former days! I always had been so very busy. There was never a moment in the day that I was not doing something. And now. . . ! However, my days of imprisonment would not be over until I had served my time; and my one purpose therefore had to be to pass away the time, somehow.

A colorful bath towel had been sent to me from home. I unraveled it and used the colored threads to embroider all my clothes. On my pajama top I conjured a window with curtains, a cyclamen, a cat, and butterflies. I kept adding to it until my pajamas were like a colorful print. It was a delightful diversion, and the days passed not too slowly. When singing, I laid aside my embroidery work; it would have been an extravagance to do two things at the same time.

I lay abed continuously. My back and arm gave me a great deal of pain, and I felt very weak. The doctor examined me and said, "I will tell you when you become tuberculous."

"It will make little difference if you tell me that two weeks too late," I replied. "It is more important that you do something now to make me better. Give me fresh air, exercise and additional food."

From then on I was given porridge and extra sandwiches from the Red Cross.

My cell was painfully colorless. My blankets were gray. The lower half of the walls were of gray tile, the upper part white. The window, high above the door, was wide and divided by bars into rectangles. Through the bars I could see the blue skies of spring and now and then a bird. I lay for hours gazing at that window, my thinking at a complete standstill. Was I becoming dull? Never before had there been such an emptiness in my life.

Suddenly I heard keys rattling outside my door. The lock grated harshly, the bolts were withdrawn, again making a noise as of violent kicking against the door; the door opened and Schenk, the *Wachtmeisterin*, and an officer entered. With a brief glance about my cell the officer seated himself on a stool beside my cot.

The brilliant colors on his uniform made me blink, stars and ribbons, and a white skull and crossbones on his cap. How strange to pick up at a glance all the details of his uniform! How smartly it was cut! Was I, perhaps, color-starved? I did not even look at his face, only at his uniform, which fascinated me. Schenk was fawningly polite to "his highness," but I was not at all impressed, and opened the conversation. I spoke German; he replied in Dutch; and then we both laughed because we knew each other's language and were just being ridiculously polite. He asked a few questions about my fellow prisoners who were arrested with me at our home. And suddenly I saw myself as I must have appeared to him. Though I had no mirror I could very well imagine how I looked.

I was lying in my slip, and my bare arms were thin. My nails were long. I had so often asked for a nail clipper, but had never been given one. Dirty, smelly blankets covered me to my waist. There were no sheets on my bed.

I felt the contrast between us. How poor I was, poorer than the poorest beggar! And that was also the way I must have looked. The officer was wealthy, well cared for, and well groomed. And yet I felt that I was the hostess, and conversed more easily than either Schenk, the *Wachtmeisterin*, or even "his highness." Were my answers judicious? I did not know. I asked him if he would not quickly release all those who had been arrested with me, as they had nothing to do with my case. Then he asked abruptly, "Are you strong enough to come to the examination room?"

How strangely that struck me! His question and intonation were in keeping with my former life back home. But they were utterly incongruous here, where everyone snarled and commanded. It touched me deeply.

"Yes, of course I am," I stammered, and actually began to look forward to the hearing.

Then he was gone, and I was once more alone. I lay thinking with amazement about this call, which had turned my thoughts toward the most dangerous experience one could have. It would not be a pleasant conversation. A hearing was a thing of terror. Whenever one of the prisoners on our corridor was taken away to appear before a *Sachbearbeiter*, or judge, we all sympathized with her intensely. The news spread from cell to cell. "Did you know that number 322 is being 'heard'?" And then everyone who could prayed for her; and when she came back, we all asked, "How was it? Did you have to confess? Did you betray anyone? Were you beaten?"

Now that dreadful experience was awaiting me. However, it still did not come as soon as I had expected. I had been in prison for two months when finally the door opened and I was ordered to get dressed. Down long, long corridors, through an office, and out of the inner gate of the prison. There the officer who had called on me in my cell was waiting for me. A long row of small rooms had been built against the outside wall. Along the corridor floor lay a magnificent heavy runner. "Stolen from the Jews" flashed through my mind. We entered the fourth room. The *Sachbearbeiter* hung his hat and holster on the hall stand.

At least I would not be faced by a threatening revolver during my hearing!

"Does it seem cold to you here? Just a minute and I'll have a fire going. You are ill, and we must not let you take cold."

Again that ordinary, friendly, human manner. It touched me more than I could understand. Was he, perhaps, just being subtle? Did he hope by his manner to betray me into revealing that which I was determined not to reveal?

I breathed a prayer, "Set a watch, O Lord, before my mouth; keep the door of my lips."

I was tense, and gripped the arms of my chair as tightly as possible. It seemed strange to be sitting in a chair again.

My *Sachbearbeiter*, Lieutenant Rahms, in his trim uniform, started building a fire. He picked up the coal out of the coal scuttle with his bare hands. "You should ask for a coal shovel for your next birthday," I remarked; and when he wiped his hands on his trousers, "Your wife should see that!"

I felt now as if I were making an ordinary call. We talked about the flowers in the garden: wind-blown tulips in a windy spot against the high prison wall.

"I planted them myself; it was such a desolate view."

Then he sat down at his desk.

"Tell me, now, exactly what you have done. It is possible that I may be able to do something for you, perhaps a great deal. But then you must not hide anything from me."

I stiffened. There it was already. All that friendliness was intended only to win my confidence. But I knew that human lives were at stake; I dared not mention any names. I had had some practice in hearings. My underground companions and I had spent many an evening conducting test hearings in which they examined me. They were clever boys, and did not spare their aunt. I knew, too, that people were often summoned at night, so I once asked a young instructor, who usually retired long after I was asleep, to waken and question me. My answers that first night were hopelessly stupid. But we continued the practice, and it became a sort of game to make each answer score a point. After ten such sessions he said, "Now you'll do; you have passed your final examination."

It had all been a game then, but, nevertheless, still a serious one because of the constant danger of its becoming a reality. That possibility had now become an actuality, and I proved to be in good trim. I even felt something of the emotion that one experiences when he has studied hard for an examination, and then is questioned on only the most elementary material.

My examiner seemed to think that our house was the center for raids on ration offices. Now, I did have a lot of illegal practices on my conscience, but in that activity I had been only indirectly involved. My answers apparently convinced him of my innocence in this respect.

Then he asked about my work among young people. I couldn't imagine what his purpose was, but it made me feel so at ease that it was no longer necessary to consider each sentence so carefully.

"What do you do with your free time?" he asked.

I told him of my efforts of evangelization among the mentally deficient in Haarlem.

"Isn't that a waste of time? It certainly is of much greater importance to convert a normal person than a feeble-minded one."

"Genuine national socialist philosophy," I thought to myself, and replied, "The Lord Jesus has other than human standards. The Bible reveals Him as one who has great love and mercy for all the lost and despised, for all who are small and weak and poor. It is possible that in His sight a mentally deficient person is of greater worth than you or I. Every human soul is valuable to Him. His love includes us all."

The man opposite me was silent. I could see that he was thinking. Then he said abruptly, "That will do for today."

He led the way back through the prison gate and down the long, long corridors. He was strangely morose. The cell door closed after me, and I was once more alone.

"How did it go?"

"Was it bad?"

"Did you mention any names?"

The questions came anxiously through the small aperture in the wall under the table. I could set their minds at ease. "No, it was not at all bad."

I told of his building a fire, and of the easy hearing.

"It's incredible! Do watch yourself. Don't trust him. Use all of your free time from now on to plan what you will say at your next hearing."

That recalled my first day in Cell 397, when I had been given the same advice. My answer then had been, "That is unnecessary, for the Lord promises us in His Word that if we are brought before rulers and kings He will give to us, through His Spirit, whatsoever we shall speak."

One of my fellow prisoners had then said, "Very well, trust that God will give you the answers in less weighty matters; but in anything as important as a hearing, I should still prefer to depend on my own reasoning." How little do they who do not know the Lord understand what peace there is in being led by an all-powerful Savior!

Now I gave the same answer, and reflected, lying abed a bit later, that the promise had been kept. It had turned out well, and I could trust in the Lord for the future also.

The next morning I was called quite early, and found my examiner himself had come to fetch me. This time he did not take me into the examination room, but kept me standing in the sun against the garden wall.

"You get far too little sunshine; we can go on with the examination here as well as inside." His kindness touched me. My imprisonment seemed not nearly so bad, now that there was one person who did not snarl at me but, on the contrary, even seemed to give some thought to what was pleasant for me.

He leaned against the wall and said, "I did not sleep all night, but thought constantly of what you told me about Jesus. Tell me more about Him." This was no mighty officer standing beside me, no powerful person who passed judgment upon the lives of others. Here was a mere man, who had been brought into touch with God and had learned his own poverty.

"Jesus Christ is a Light, come into the world in order that everyone who believes in Him need not remain in darkness. Is there darkness in your life?"

"There is great darkness in my life. When I go to bed at night I dare not think of the moment that I must awaken in the morning. When I awaken, I dread the day. I hate my work. I have a wife and children in Bremen, but do not even know if they are alive. Who knows, a bomb may have shattered them last night. Yes, there is darkness in my life."

"Jesus bore your sins also on the cross. Surrender yourself completely to Him, and there will be light in your life. There is no darkness so great that Jesus cannot dispel it."

I spoke to him at great length about eternal things. Later, we went into the examination room; and when my protocol was finally made up, I signed it. Before typing it he read it aloud to me. The concluding paragraph of the *procès-verbal* was noteworthy:

> She plans to continue in the future what she has done in the past, because she wants to help all those who appeal to her for aid, regardless of their race or creed. She is determined to do this because she is obedient to the command of Christ to love God and her neighbors.

As he brought me back to my cell he said, suddenly, "I cannot understand how you can believe that there is a God, for if there is, why should He permit you, a brave woman, to be imprisoned?"

"God never makes a mistake. There is much that we shall not understand until later. But this is no problem to me. It is God's will that I should for a time be alone with Him."

After I had been questioned for several days, it was my sister Betsie's turn. She had little to confess. I myself had considerably more on my conscience, while she knew of nothing but assistance to the Jews. Her examination, nevertheless, lasted four days. It was one continued witness to, and discourse about, Jesus. At the close of the first day's hearing, she said to her interrogator, "It was very much worthwhile to speak of these things with each other; but it is still more important to pray. Have you any objection to my praying for you?"

"No," said the officer, "you may do so." And Betsie prayed with him. She was childlike in her simplicity. Each day thereafter, her examination was closed with prayer.

When Peter, the youngest son of my other sister, was brought in for hearing, the conversation again turned to the same subject.

"What do you think?" asked the *Sachbearbeiter*. "Do you believe there will be a better time after this war?"

"No, not until Jesus returns; then only will everything be as it should."

"You may be right about that."

Then the boy asked, "Are you ready for that day?"

There was no reply.

After having been questioned, nearly all of those arrested with us were released. One of the boys, Betsie and I remained. What our sentence was, we never learned.

Letters

A letter was placed in the small opening in my door. I seized it and felt more nervous than at any time before. My first contact with home! I had tried consistently not to think too much about home. Now I was to learn what their situation was. It was a letter from my married sister, who had meanwhile been released.

I read my letter.

"Will you be brave, Corrie? I have news that is very hard to write to you. Father survived his arrest by only ten days. He is now home."

Though I could have surmised it, it was still a severe blow, and I burst into tears. It was the first time I had cried. A great longing to have someone near me impelled me to call the *Wachtmeisterin*. I pressed the emergency bell, which caused a small board to fall with a great clatter.

"Mopje," a small and fairly human *Wachtmeisterin*, appeared at the opening in my door.

"Please stay with me a few minutes. I have just received word that my father has passed away. Please do not leave me."

"Wait just a minute, I'll be right back," was her reply. A few minutes later she came back with a bottle of sedative. I refused to take it; and then she sat down beside me. At first she was embarrassed and silent. Then she burst out, "If you had not done the wrong things for which you were sent here, you would have been with your father, and he would not have died alone. It is all your own fault. You really shouldn't cry. You should be happy that your father lived so long. My father was only fifty-six when he died."

What a comforter! "The tender mercies of the wicked are cruel" (Prov. 12:10).

I was glad that she did not stay long. How foolish of me to have desired the companionship of a human being!

E. ten Boom, Cell 312

Dear Nollie,

I am very well now. Since my letter of April 14 things have been better, and I feel well, both physically and spiritually. The atmosphere in our cell is fine. My soul is very calm. I have fortunately recovered from the shocks of the past month. I have disciplined myself to think almost exclusively about my cellmates and our cell life, sharing intensely in all of its ups and downs. At first I prayed for everybody and everything, but later I learned not to do that. I had to confine myself to thinking about texts and meditations, psalms and hymns, which I could remember. Of some of them, I remember only fragments, but I enjoy even the fragments. Thinking of these things through the long weeks of waiting brought me peace. And then on April 28 another prisoner, originally from Haarlem, entered our cell. Last Tuesday we had a conversation about Haarlem which gave me a renewed perspective of my whole manner of life. Then on Wednesday came your letter. What a joy!

I was questioned on Thursday, Friday, Saturday, and Monday, and on Monday signed the procès-verbal. The hearings were one continued miracle. Your prayers, as always, surrounded me. Every preceding night the Lord revealed to me what I should say. It was not so much a hearing as a glorious conversation to the honor of Christ. Of course I had to explain the motivating impulse of all our activities, and that gave me an opportunity to witness to the love and saving grace of our Savior. I do that constantly in my cell also.

I heard almost immediately that Peter and Willem were free, and that Father had been released on March 9. And what a release that was! The Lord leads me every minute and every second. That gives me courage. Now I have only to wait. I yearn for you, for freedom, and for work. I sleep as I have never slept before in my life. The friendship among us in our cell is so close that I have invited all of my cellmates, without exception, into our home.

I am fortunately given porridge every day. And I have had three injections. Three cheers for the Red Cross!

Remember now: Pray and give thanks.

Yours, Betsie

C. ten Boom, Cell 384

Dear Nollie and Other Dear Ones,

I received your letter on May 3. At first I was grief-stricken, but now I am quite comforted. Father can now sing:

"I cannot live without Thee, Thou Jesus my Lord,

And I am Thine forever; be Thy Name adored."

How beautiful his voice must sound! I think it is wonderful for him. When I think of his nine days in prison I turn quickly to the present and absorb myself in thoughts of his happiness. He now sees the solution of all earthly problems. On my cell wall is written: "Not lost but gone before."

His death has left a great void in my life. For the love and help I gave to him, the Lord will provide another outlet. What I received from him cannot be replaced. But what a privilege it is that we have enjoyed him, consciously and intensely, for so many years! I was upset for a few days, but that is past. For a while the sense of strain was so great I did not dare think about things, and it is so difficult to escape thinking when one is entirely alone. Now that is all past, and I think a great deal about the future. I am making plans and am quite calm.

How good the Savior is to me! He not only helps carry my burden; He carries me also. I have signed my protocol. I hope to get home this month; if not then, in God's good time. Do not feel badly, Nollie, that I am alone. The Savior supplies every need. All that I lack He gives in rich abundance and beyond measure. Yes, Nollie, your way, too, is hard; but the Lord will give you courage to help you through this difficult time. I pray much for you. All of you pray much for me also. Greetings, dear children and friends. God bless you all.

I am feeling fairly well, so do not worry about me. The hearing was not at all bad. The Lord gave me great assurance and boldness to witness for Him. I am not afraid. The Savior will never leave me in the lurch, not in that respect either.

Yours, Corrie

Company in the Cell

Tiny ants were running about near the door of my cell. They had selected their own well-defined territory, and in it a fixed little path. I fed them daily with bread crumbs. I was now given Red Cross sandwiches every day, and it was a recurrent source of pleasure. Usually there was some small surprise in the packet—a couple of lemon drops, a few peppermints, or a bit of rock candy. I wondered if the Red Cross workers knew how much good these small kindnesses did me. It touched me so, just by way of contrast to the wickedness of those who guarded me. One day there was egg in my sandwich. The crumbs I threw to the floor were bestormed by my little ants. Bits of egg, six times as large as they themselves, were laboriously dragged up the wall to a stone ledge near the door. I watched them for hours at a time, and swept very carefully around their small domain. I was fond of my tiny cellmates.

The loneliness was hard to bear. Just to see no one but these cross and unfriendly caretakers was a punishment in itself. When I set my *kubel* and dirty water outside, none of the cell doors adjoining mine was opened, for fear I might see one of my neighbors. Why such great secrecy? I wondered.

Then one kind day my door opened and a Jewish woman was pushed inside. Astonished, I welcomed her and tried to help her through those first bad moments. She had brought nothing with her, so I gave her part of my wardrobe, which had been replenished by packages from home. What a joy to have someone near me! We talked a great deal, so much that I was exhausted by the end of the day. I was no longer used to talking. She was a friendly woman, but greatly distressed and worried. Her husband, whom she had been nursing night and day, was a diabetic.

"He cannot get along without me," she moaned. "I know they will not give him his injections. I have the insulin in my suitcase."

I could scarcely restrain her from ringing for her suitcase. I knew that she would never again see anything of those well-filled bags, but she couldn't understand that. She talked tiresomely for hours about the luxury she had had to leave behind. Still, I enjoyed her presence. Now there was someone for me to love. That very day another package arrived, and now I had someone with whom I could share it. It had been such a cheerless thing to enjoy the contents of a parcel alone. Mealtimes, too, had an air about them now. This woman was a timid and frightened newcomer, compared to me. I tried to initiate her into prison ways.

After a few days she was subjected to a brief hearing, and from then on was tormented by the awful fear of "the transport."

Looking up from my bed, I saw that she was lying with her head on her arms on the table. Now and then she moaned, "Will they torture me to death? Will they put me into the gas chamber?" I tried to tell her of God's love, but she was impervious to comfort. I was not lonely now, but was alone with someone who had been sentenced to death and who had given way completely to fear. I prayed constantly for her and struggled with the Lord for her salvation.

Then one night a Jewish transport went out. Merciless lights were turned on; she was given half an hour to dress, and she left my cell, one mass of despair. Once more I was alone; but my struggle for her soul went on for a long time afterward.

"The General"

A new *Wachtmeisterin* appeared in the door of my cell. She was the new *ober*. She had at first been head of a prison in Berlin, then in Oslo, and had now come to bring order among the undisciplined horde of Scheveningen. Like a whirlwind she cleared up one bad condition after another. Every two weeks we were to have a clean sheet. And I had not seen a sheet these past six weeks, even though I had been so very ill. We were to have regular airings. And I had been in this cell for fifty days without ever having been outside, except for that one trip to the consultation bureau. Were conditions going to be better? Was this *Wachtmeisterin* going to be more human? I had never before seen such an evil-looking woman. Her features were regular, but she had cold, piercing eyes that looked capable of petrifying one if he were to cross her.

Never had I seen a harder or more cruel face than that of this woman, with her tall, erect figure. I had to jump up from my bed and stand at attention. Without a word she went through my poor small cell. Off came the red paper, shading my lamp. Canisters from my last precious package from home she turned upside down until cookies, vitamins, and sandwich spreads lay in a confused heap on the table. I had to empty the jar of apple butter myself. I didn't dare ask her where to put it, but just grabbed a piece of toilet paper and shook it out on that with trembling fingers. She pulled the blankets off the cot and looked under the mattress to see if I'd hidden anything there. Fortunately she did not see my Gospels.

This woman frightened me. When the door closed behind her I fell back onto my mattress, before trying to clear up the mess on the table, and listened to what was going on in the next cells. She "tidied up" all along the line. Colors vanished. Cells were left more desolate than before. An evil spirit was blowing through the prison.

She was usually silent. When she did speak it was in sharp, lancet-like commands. I heard her scold even an aged woman who had not jumped instantly to attention. And I was reminded of my mother. I always felt badly when the aged people here were treated roughly. I had not yet learned that old age was despised under this regime.

Later on I would come to know "The General" at close quarters in the barracks of Vught. But whether there was anything good, anything human, in her character would always remain a mystery to me.

3

Light Through Iron Bars at Vught

The Arrival

E veryone put on their own clothing!"
What could be going on? It was now June; I had been in Scheveningen prison for four months. Whisperings of an expected invasion flew back and forth through secret cracks and holes in the walls. The women guards had seemed excited all day. Could it be . . . ?

Was it possible that liberation was at hand? Why should the men be putting on their own clothing?

An order was shouted down the corridor, but I failed to understand it. Others told me through the crevice in the wall that everyone must get ready to leave and take all his belongings with him.

What an interruption in the dull routine of prison life! Nervously we started packing, hurrying for fear we might not be ready on time. And then it was actually hours before the order came, "Everybody out!"

There we stood, five abreast. For the first time I was allowed to see my fellow prisoners. The guards were all so very busy they could not keep us from talking.

Then we were loaded into huge vans and buses and brought to a small station outside of The Hague. And there I saw, among all the other prisoners, Betsie. A great longing took possession of me. As we were getting on the train, we pressed toward each other and succeeded in getting into the same coach. There we sat, side by side, talking. For more than fifty years we had lived together in almost perfect harmony; and now we had been separated for so long and under such circumstances! Words were unnecessary. We sat hand in hand, "the lovebirds," as one woman teasingly called us.

At four o'clock in the morning we arrived at Vught, sixty miles inland from The Hague. The guards were nervous. All of the women and half the men from the Scheveningen prison were here; and there were not enough guards. Several prisoners had, indeed, succeeded in escaping from the train.

We alighted at a spot in the middle of a wood. Powerful searchlights played upon us, creating weird shadows of trees, carts, and guards. All around us gleamed the weapons of the soldiers, their guns leveled menacingly at us. Again we were ordered to "fall in."

I had put our clothing and the leftovers from the last parcels into a pillowcase, which began to tear just as we were being driven along an open stretch of land. Because I did not dare stop even for a second, I tied it up with the belt of my coat as we marched along.

Through the darkness they drove us on. Cursing, storming and abuse was all we heard. One of the soldiers kicked some of the women in the back because they swerved to avoid a puddle of water. O night of terror! But Betsie and I were together, together! And the fearful march came to an end when we were brought into a large hall, furnished with benches without backs. There we were left from between four and five in the morning until four in the afternoon, without food and without supervision. The latter we did not mind, for it was a faint suggestion of freedom, and we were together. But less pleasant moments arrived. The women were made to undress, were sent into the showers twenty at a time.

Soldiers were walking around staring at the undressed women who had to wait for their showers. Betsie and I threw our arms about each other and pleaded, "O Lord, not that."

"Stop bathing," came the command. There were not enough gowns.

We shed tears of gratitude. Our turn had not yet come; and when, ten days later, we were given our prison gowns we were alone with the friendly girls of the dressing room, and there was nothing unpleasant or mean about it. God answers prayers.

I was no longer in solitary confinement, but with a hundred and fifty other women. But their griefs and sorrows, too, were within the same walls with me. And there was so much grief and sorrow among us. A sweet young Jewess came to me and said, "Can you comfort me? I am so frightened."

Betsie prayed with her. We both felt that a new era had begun for us. We now had association with many people; we would have to share in their grief, but we would also be privileged to help and encourage them.

We were now in Vught, but not yet in the camp. There the women wore a uniform of blue overalls, with a red stripe down the back and an attractive blue-and-white polka-dotted kerchief. Here we were still allowed to wear our own clothing.

We had some things in common with the others: we were constantly in the company of all sorts of people of greatly divergent characters, and there was never a moment's opportunity of being alone.

Discipline had been more rigid in the Scheveningen Barracks. It was considered a sort of probationary period. Later I observed that the food here was of much poorer quality than in the camp proper. Nor were we allowed to receive parcels or mail. Camp prisoners were outside a good deal, while our airing consisted of a brief march around the barracks. And even this privilege was taken away for the slightest offense.

We were all housed together in a separate barrack, consisting of one large room. In it were tables and benches. All day long we sat side by side at the tables, doing nothing. The women guards from Scheveningen were supposed to direct us. But they were stupid, untrained women of the lower classes. They could easily control their prisoners when they were kept in restraint behind bolted cell doors; but here, where there were several hundreds of women who, in spite of prison discipline, possessed a certain degree of power against them, these guards had not the faintest conception of psychology, leadership or organization.

I recalled the time when I was on the board of a girls' organization and had to inspect their camps.

"A poorly directed camp with totally incompetent leaders" would certainly have been my estimate of the Scheveningen Barracks. The women guards were conscious of their weakness, and tried, by way of compensation, to demonstrate their authority by constant threats of severe punishment.

When we marched I enjoyed the exercise and the few minutes out of doors. Betsie was too weak and unpracticed to keep in step, and frequently fell out. A corridor attendant was in command. She was a girl from Sarasani's Circus. I could forgive her for the mistakes she made in her commands, but I did resent her constant spying and reporting of small punishable offenses. In the barracks opposite us were the men from Scheveningen. Many of these women had husbands, sons or sweethearts among them, and would try to catch a glimpse of them, to call out a word of encouragement, or simply wave to them, all of which was, of course, strictly forbidden.

For hours we now sat side by side at the tables doing nothing. Boredom gradually crept over us. There was grumbling and criticizing, and the conversations were no longer stimulating. The corridor attendants from Scheveningen took charge of us when "their highnesses," the guards, were off duty. Most of them were attractive young girls, fellow prisoners, who had great responsibilities and who were frequently not equal to their difficult tasks.

But now Betsie had an idea. She organized a society. How could it be otherwise; so many Hollanders together and no society? Rules for membership were very simple: "Whoever wishes to become a member must promise to do his utmost not to grumble or complain, or speak ill of anyone, but only to speak encouragingly to others. Next, she must resolve to obey all orders of the corridor attendants."

A small group of us agreed to pray daily that the atmosphere would improve and remain good.

At six o'clock we had to go to bed. We were not even allowed to wash ourselves or brush our teeth. Then the guards would disappear, leaving the Sarasani girl[14] in charge. We lay abed talking for a long time, for it was much too early to sleep, and there was plenty of time. What fine people some of these women were! I made friends with several of them.

During the day "The General" was often with us. I was conscious of my fear of her. She was stronger than the other women, who apparently had difficulty keeping order among us. Roll call under her was sheer misery because of her sarcastic comments, her cruel face, and her merciless punishments. She made us stand for hours. A pregnant woman once fainted, striking her head on a bench as she fell; The General looked on unmoved.

One day the doctor came, gave me a superficial examination, and said, "You have tuberculosis; you must stay abed from now on."

After roll call I went to The General and asked her if I might not lie close to the window, since I was no longer allowed to be up during the day.

"You are going to work today, and work hard, then your tuberculosis will disappear."

I really felt well enough to be up, but the ugliness of her answer hurt me.

Threats

Just as we were standing in file to go with the ropemaking crew, Betsie and I were summoned by The General. She had several paper forms in her hand.

"You are free," whispered a corridor attendant. "That pink form always indicates that a prisoner is to be released."

Joy welled up within me. But what a pity I had to leave the rest behind!

I tried to console them. "You will certainly go home soon also; the war cannot last much longer."

We divided most of our possessions among them; we would soon have everything we needed, for we would be at home with family and friends. . . .

They were moved, as they said good-bye, for they were so genuinely happy for us. A few doubted that we would really be released.

We followed The General to an office. The weather was delightful, and Betsie and I walked hand in hand. Personal effects, taken from us upon entering the camp, were now returned to us—watches, rings, and money. Money! That had to do with a normal society! Pretty soon we would buy railway tickets with it and travel toward home! We walked a great distance to the building at the main camp exit. Here we were kept standing in line with ten men. There were now four of us women. The view of flowers and shrubs was beautiful. Then I saw two men being chased about the area. An officer on a bicycle was making them run at full speed from one barracks to another. There was something repulsive in the expression on the face of the officer; he laughed as if he was enjoying himself immensely. How cruel laughter can be!

One of the four women was briefly questioned and inadvertently revealed that she was a Jewess. She was taken out next to the great gate and made to stand facing the wall with her back toward us. She was thin and spindly and very scantily clad. Her whole bearing expressed unspeakable desolation. Where would she be taken? What a profoundly unfortunate human being it was standing there! She was at that moment a symbol of the suffering of her people.

"How long, O Lord? Oh, have mercy on Thine ancient people Israel," I pleaded.

One of the men beside me said suddenly, "If any one of you can pray, you had better do so now; not one of us knows what is going to become of him."

"Yes, we can pray," said Betsie. "Let's do so. But, really, we thought we were about to be released. Isn't that true?"

"No," said the man, and there was sympathy in his voice, "you will not be released. You will be brought into the bunkers,[15] or even worse; no one knows."

"Evidently the Lord still has work for us to do here," said Betsie, bravely. And a few minutes later she began to sing. There was no guard in the vicinity, so no one forbade it. At that moment I experienced a peculiar sense of contradiction. I was enjoying thoroughly the glorious weather, the flowers and shrubs, and the wide blue sky, and also the singing; but at the same time, I was conscious of an intense feeling of strain.

Betsie was singing:

> *Let us bring all our homage to Jesus,*
> *And sing of His love and His might,*
> *Great things He will certainly give him*
> *Who makes the Lord's will his delight.*
> *I do not fear the dim tomorrow,*
> *For my Savior holds my hand.*
> *Strong in Him, I turn from sorrow*
> *And I face the unknown land.*
>
> *May I go on ever certain*
> *That Thou doest what is best!*
> *May I carry one day's burden*
> *With a quiet strength and rest.*

"Fall in," came the snarling command.

Beside me now stood a fellow prisoner in a badly torn uniform of the mounted police. He took over Betsie's pack, which she was about to drop.

"My heart is beating so strangely," she said. I felt her pulse; it was very weak and irregular.

We were brought to another office, where our possessions were once more taken from us—my Bible I had hidden under my dress. Was this whole demonstration intended merely to vex and torment us? Why not tell us at once where we were going? A little later we were brought into the inner courtyard of the bunkers. On three sides were gloomy cells with small barred windows, shaded by sloping little roofs, to let in as little light as possible. I knew that atrocities had been committed here. Women had been locked in these cells and smothered to death.

Here we were kept standing a long, long time. I looked at the men standing beside us. They had strong faces. I could see that concern was written on some of them, but also a courageous acceptance of impending danger or death. What good Netherlanders these were, at whose side I was called upon to fight this battle!

"Lord, help me to be brave," I prayed.

High in the air an English plane drew a long white line against the sky.

The threat of the bunker was averted. The end of that long day of suspense did not bring us the freedom we so longed for, but brought us into the camp at Vught.

It was already going on toward evening. The strain of standing and marching had lasted almost the entire day, and we were dead tired when finally we reached the barracks. A friendly young girl welcomed us and invited us to be seated beside her at the table.

Sunday

It was our first Sunday in the camp at Vught. We worked until twelve o'clock; then came roll call and freedom for the rest of the day. The weather was glorious. What a luxury to be outside! Betsie and I walked just for the pleasure of it, along the barbed wire fence and between the barracks. How beautiful the skies of Brabant were! A girl came up to us and invited us to attend a worship service. There, on a plot of grass between two barracks, was a group of people gathered about a woman, listening as she read to them from the Bible. We seated ourselves on the edge of a gutter that ran along the barracks. The woman next read a sermon, and then we sang. I felt deeply moved. I was once more with other children of God. There was reverence on the faces of those about me. The loneliness of the cell was forever past.

They asked me to lead them in thanksgiving. As I prayed a great joy filled my heart. How wonderful it was to speak to the Lord together, to give expression to our common need! Never before had I prayed as now. There was so much sorrow among these prisoners, who had had to leave husbands and children and other loved ones behind, and above whose heads still hung so dire a threat. And I spoke to One who understood, who knew us and loved us. On Him I cast all our burdens.

Afterwards they asked me to lead the next week's service. I did so, and also arranged a discussion group for the evening. I was accustomed to doing that frequently in our youth clubs. I would then prepare a few questions on some subject and let the group answer them. My purpose in the discussion group here was primarily to release their thinking from the narrow confines of camp life. The great danger of all institutions is that they tend to become small communities by themselves. The same thing was evident here—thinking narrowed down, conversation deteriorated, and only camp interests were talked about. I inquired at the Philips office if anyone would type several copies of the discussion outline for me, and a gentleman sitting there at a typewriter did so very neatly. I asked one of the girls who he was and learned that he was one of the prisoners, a professor.

My discussion outline was as follows:

Our Responsibility After This Prison Camp Experience

1. How can we gain the courage and strength necessary to face the problems?

2. Is it necessary to start thinking now about our lives after camp?
3. Will God expect from us any specific accomplishment?
4. For whom shall we be able and obligated to do something?
5. What categories of persons will most likely have difficulties?
6. What can we do for:
   a. those who return from imprisonment and find themselves without families;
   b. those who have lost homes and furnishings;
   c. those who have become unbalanced;
   d. young people who have problems of adjustment on returning to a normal society;
   e. the military;
   f. the prisoners;
   g. the defeated enemy—have we any responsibilities toward them?
7. What is the most important thing that can help all of these people?

What a task it was to lead the discussion! In our clubs at home, though we frequently differed in inclinations, we were agreed on the most important matters. Here the people were of widely divergent views of life. A Hollander claimed theology was the solution; some inclined towards abstruse philosophy; others theorized superficially. By no means did they all understand one another. As a discussion it was a fiasco; but I had at least succeeded in extending the range of our thinking and speaking beyond the boundaries of barbed wire.

A Belgian Tells

We were sitting on the sands of Vught. Nearby were shrubs and birches, many birches. Birds were singing. Beyond the little sand-plot that constituted our garden was a double barbed wire barricade. But through it we could see a wide expanse of meadow-lands, a farm, and here and there small woodlands. And overhead was the wide blue sky of Brabant.

A Belgian woman was speaking. She and her family had been cruelly driven about, from Belgium to Germany, and then from one prison to another, and finally to Vught. It had been a relief to be here. We had fairly good lodgings and sufficient fresh air, and the summer was bright and sunny.

"We were in a small prison in Belgium when we were bombed. Nearer and nearer we heard the bombs fall. Suddenly we heard the kind voice of our priest. He often came to comfort us. He would stand just outside where we could all understand him.

"'My children,' he now called us, 'danger is approaching. It may be only a few minutes before your last hour will have struck. Prepare yourselves for death.

"'You are now face to face with death and standing in the presence of God. Consider your extremity; repent fervently of your sins.

"'Pray with our divine Savior, who died for us on the cross: "Lord, into Thy hands do I commit my spirit."

"'Remember the words of Jesus: "I am the resurrection and the life: he that believeth in Me, though he were dead, yet shall he live; and whosoever liveth and believeth in Me, shall never die."

"'*Misere mei Deus*: have mercy on me, O Lord, according to Thy loving kindness.'

"His words were lost in a terrific crash, as a bomb struck right beside us. I was prepared to die, and waited. The windows were all broken, the shattered glass lying all about us. We remained on our knees, and thoughts were on our last moments. When the din subsided a bit, we again heard the calm voice of the priest:

"'Almighty God be merciful unto you, pardon your sins, and lead you into eternal life. Amen.'

"Those were his last words. Another crash close by caused me to lose consciousness. When I came to, I was still in my cell, and everything was quiet. My cellmates lifted me up so I could look out of the window. I saw a ruined city. All the houses around the prison were destroyed. The only building left standing was the prison itself. And in front of our cell lay the priest, the crucifix clasped in his dead hands."

Slave Market

We had been ordered to report for the Philips crew, and were sitting in the entrance of Barracks 4, waiting to be directed to our places. The younger women all had been called for that work before. Most of those here now were around forty, and some of them still older. There was only disdain for age in this place.

We were sitting along the sides of the hall, waiting, when a group of men entered and remained standing in the center. One of them was the *Oberkapo*,[16] a negroid type with a thick, protruding lower lip which gave his entire face a cruel expression. He had already beaten many a Jew to death. Earlier in his life he had been sentenced to sixteen years in prison for murder, and he had now accumulated a lot of experience in German concentration camps. Here he was at the head of the prisoners working at Philips. Some of the other men might have been pleasant persons, we didn't know. But as they looked us over, gauged our possibilities, and discussed us among themselves, I felt very much like a slave in the slave market. With some of the others I was pointed out and called forward. A slight shiver ran down my spine, but at the same time the entire episode seemed unreal to me.

Now I was standing before them. If they considered me too old for factory work at Philips I would very likely have to twist rope. I could not say that one task would be any more pleasant than the other. But this inspection, I felt, was humiliating. How independent I had always been!

"Another shall gird thee and carry thee whither thou wouldest not" (John 21:18). "I must be more humble." I had told myself that often enough. Now I was being humbled. But it was all right. I was in training.

I was approved and sent to the Philips factory.

Philips Work Crew

A young man took us to Barracks 35, where there were long rows of workbenches, one after the other. I was given easy but monotonous work, measuring small glass rods. I looked around me. There was a pleasant atmosphere in the room. The foreman was a fellow prisoner who had formerly been the principal of a high school, and he did not fail to do credit to his background. He had created an atmosphere of refinement in these factory surroundings. He took care of us in a fatherly way. I felt more like one of his students than like a factory hand. He soon observed my interest in the work of others. Measuring glass rods was hopelessly monotonous, and so I tried my hand at the more interesting work of others, soldering and mounting radio parts. The foreman remarked with amazement, "You are the first woman prisoner who has shown any interest in the work."

"Yes, but you see," I replied, "I am a watchmaker."

When he heard that, he at once gave me different work, checking relay switches. It was fairly precise work, but not as interesting as repairing watches.

I adjusted myself to the work rather quickly, though eleven hours at a workbench was much longer than I had been accustomed to at home. And in the cell I had lain abed the entire day. There was not the slightest possibility of that now. It was a tremendous change for me, but I was thankful for the diversion that the work afforded. Vught was much more bearable than the cell at Scheveningen. I enjoyed the outdoor air and the pleasant association with my fellow prisoners, among whom were some splendid persons. During lunchtime we were permitted to stay outside. And it was wonderful to have the sunlight and green grass, and space about me. From my workbench I could look out over the street which the *Aufseherinnen*[17] and officers took when they stopped in to check on us. Whenever I saw these dangers approaching I would call out, "thick clouds," our prearranged warning; and suddenly everyone would be hard at work. Books which were being read disappeared; handwork and letters were quickly hidden. One day a very corpulent *Aufseherin* entered and heard the cry, "thick clouds." She thought it was a reflection on her person, and was furious. From then on we used the innocuous word "fifteen" as our signal. "I've assembled fifteen dials."

Frequently, as we marched to work in the morning, we could see the area where thousands of men prisoners were standing in ranks. All of them had their heads shaved. Roll call had usually just ended, and the men were falling into ranks according to work crews. This was done in double-quick time; and the sight of all those bald heads, moving and milling around, reminded me of a sackful of peas being stirred about.

En route we passed several small woods. The sun had just risen, and its rays fell obliquely on leaves and grass that sparkled with a million drops of dew. I enjoyed that walk.

At 6:45 we arrived at the Philips division of Camp Vught. On a side path I waited for Leny Franse, a friend of mine from Haarlem. Together we took our morning stroll along "the sands." The sky was magnificently colored, the sun just above the horizon, and the clouds from east to west delicately tinted in pastels. Leny told me that she had just received word that all of her possessions, including her house, had been taken from her. She was brave, and surrendered herself definitely to God's will. She told me about her small son, Robert, who so trustingly placed his grief in God's hands. We then repeated together "The Lord is my help and my strength." Those five minutes together each morning were precious to us.

Long lines of men were marching past us, in uniform prison-striped suits and shaved heads, and yet each one distinctively his own type. In the factory entrance stood a man and a woman, both Belgians. Back home their respective mates were waiting for them; but here they stood with their lips together. Yonder were Jaap and Sena with their arms about each other. Sena ran a bar in Rotterdam; Jaap was a sailor.

The foul air of the workroom rushed at us when we opened the door. All the windows were closed, and we hurried to open them and let the fresh morning air pour in. As we entered we saw that Muller, the chief officer, had been inspecting drawers and cupboards. On the floor lay a chaotic mass of refuse: butter, socks, a tomato, bread, broken glass, etc. Bah! What a vandal! In disgust I sat down at my workbench and laid my head on my arms; I didn't want to see the disorder. Besides, I was tired. We had got up at 4:45, and that is a bit early. I dozed off for a few minutes' sleep.

The Dormitory

It was evening. There were one hundred and twenty prisoners in our dormitory. Looking up, I gazed over a sea of beds. Such merry goings-on—eating, talking and laughing! But it was not long before everything quieted down. An eleven-hour workday was fatiguing; add to that an annoyingly long roll call, and everyone was dead tired.

All were asleep. Here and there someone snored. British planes were roaring overhead. Gray light appeared on the horizon. A searchlight from the sentry box cast a piercing beam through the dormitory. The sentries shouted at one another and called out that it was a quarter to two. They were always restless when planes were overhead and gave vent to their uneasiness by being noisy.

I closed my eyes and dreamed of a bed with sheets. I walked through our house in the Barteljorisstraat and ran my hand over the newel post; I walked across the living room and threw a piece of wood on the fire. Then I looked up at Father's portrait, and tears welled up under my closed eyelids.

Parcel Number Twelve

Vught was a place of many contrasts. Parcels had arrived. Betsie's and mine stood between us on a bench. A wealth of good things came out of it: sugar, butter, and even luxuries like cake, biscuits and sweets—all delicious things thought of and packed by loving hearts and hands. Even the return address suggested hope: "In case of eventual release, return to Haarlem."

It was a small feast in the midst of a somber prison camp. Like children, we arranged the little boxes and bags about us, sampling generously of this and that, and giving here and there to others, debating who most needed a certain article. The sandwiches were unusually well filled, and were quickly tucked away in our "stowaway bag" for a generous second breakfast for tomorrow.

The feast had begun in the *Schreibstube*.[18] The *Aufseherin* had taken everything out, piece by piece, had run her long knife through the butter to see if there were any messages hidden in it, and cut the cake into pieces. The neatly packed box had quickly become messy. But everything in it seemed to smile. We repacked it neatly, and thought of those at home who had planned it. It seemed to give us new courage, and we told each other that we should very well be able to hold out until the great day of deliverance came.

From the bunkers we heard a salvo of shots!

Disciplinary March

It was a shining summer day. As we left the factory and fell in line one person was tardy. The penalty was to march from twelve o'clock until one. A fire brigade *Kapo*,[19] an attractive young fellow, was to lead us. I believe he was a seaman by trade. He had a rod in his hand, but we were not afraid of him. We enjoyed ourselves doubly. The march took us through a section of the camp we had not yet seen. First we passed an airplane graveyard, *Die Luftwaffe*; here, men from the guardhouse dismantled the planes that had crashed. Then we followed a lane overlooking a grain field, and in the distance we could see a church spire. What a joy! We sang as we marched. Johanna, the *Aufseherin*, was furious. She simply did not know what to think of these Holland women. They actually enjoyed their punishment! We were spirited and cheerful, and someone started singing:

> *We never let our courage fall,*
> *We hold our heads up high.*
> *They never, never will prevail,*
> *No matter how they try.*
> *Onward we press, our word is 'yes,'*
> *Heads up, you women of Vught, heads up.*

"What building is that?" I asked.

"That is a crematorium," said someone, looking apprehensively at Mrs. Akkerman. Her son had been shot to death just the week before. He was twenty years old.

Letters

Pretexts for punishment were avidly seized upon in Vught. The *Aufseherinnen* tried to make us feel that we were far too well treated as prisoners. If a couple of beds were not made according to the rule, we were all punished by a mail and parcel ban. What a severe punishment that was! No contact with the outside world! But one woman found a way out; she bribed an S.S. soldier to post our letters for us outside the camp. So the letters we now wrote were not censored. It was, of course, a dangerous procedure. If one letter were intercepted, the penalty would be at least prolonged imprisonment. But we took that risk.

Vught, July 13, 1944

Dear All of You,

At the moment we are under mail and parcel ban. Why, no one knows. But I shall continue writing. Life here is hard, but we are given sufficient grace for it all, and are being wonderfully sustained. We rise at five in the morning, have roll call at six, and at six thirty start work. Evenings we are already in bed at nine. Corrie and I are together much of the time. We get back from work at seven in the evening, and then have our supper together quietly. We are enjoying the beauties of nature tremendously. Such skies and clouds! Everyone continues to be full of courage. On the whole, the atmosphere is excellent, calm but spirited. Many of those around us are friendly. Do go on praying for us. We experience its effects every hour and every minute. In regard to our release, I am perfectly at ease; that will come in the Lord's own time. Meanwhile, grace has been given me to stay here, although I naturally long for you all. But this life is infinitely better than that in the cell. Although we are receiving no parcels, the Lord sees to it that we have enough.

Be of good courage! Jesus is Victor!

Your Betsie

Dear Ones,

You will certainly ask what we have done to deserve the ban on parcels. It is a collective punishment. In our barracks the beds were not neatly made; too many things had been hidden under the mattresses; and, moreover, a few of the Stootploeg[20] had talked through the window and across the barbed-wire barricade with kapos. We all suffer the punishment together. The ban will be on until September 5. After that, send us especially some heavy sweaters; as the mornings get colder, we shall not be dressed warmly enough. We now have roll call before sunrise. How beautiful the skies are then! But we sometimes shiver from the cold when the mornings are misty and autumnal. Just now we are having a heat wave. How I long for cool sheets—and for a few other things! Do you think the end of the war is approaching? It would be the most wonderful thing if all of us here could be saved at the same time. It seems to us that conditions in society are none too attractive just now either. But if they were ten times worse, we would still want to go home.

We are doing well. Today is Betsie's birthday; and what a day it is, compared with my last birthday! I lay sick and alone, and was being punished with kalte-kost because I had talked. I was given no dinner, no airing, no books; and everyone snarled at me. I was feeling sick and unhappy when the doctor came to give me an injection. When I told him it was my birthday, he gave me a hearty handshake. He himself was a prisoner. Never have I appreciated a handshake more.

The next day a corridor girl came to my door and congratulated me for Aukje.[21] *At that time I also heard for the first time where Betsie was. It was my first contact with her. Now she waits for me every evening, and we sleep together. Last night we awakened at the same time from the terrific roar of a tremendous number of planes flying over Vught. There seemed to be thousands of them.*

At noon I sleep for an hour in the sun. The skies here are marvelous with heavenly beauty. We have enough to eat, are well, have pleasant work, and many friends and acquaintances. I am burned brown from the sun, and even Betsie's face is brown. She looks much better than some time ago, and at least ten years younger. The hand in which I had neuritis is nearly well, and I have gained considerable weight.

I was stung on the leg by a wasp and got a pass to go to the Sanitäter, *a few barracks farther up. He gave me a compress with eau de cologne. The nicest part of it was the walk. In the Philips factory area we are not allowed outside of our own barracks without a pass.*

Do not worry that we may not have enough food. The Lord takes constant care of us. If we have nothing left, someone is sure to give us something; for instance, I went to the hospital for Vitamin B, and the cleaning woman gave me half a cake.

Did you know that Leny Franse is here in Barracks 24? Her husband is in 23.

Have you any idea whether our prison term ends on September 1 or December 8?

Everyone here says that six months at Vught is the minimum term. If my time at Scheveningen is included my term should be up on September 1. God knows the way, and we are resting in His will. I think about home more than Betsie does. She has pleasant work, mending with the sewing machine, but she does at times grow very tired. Rereading my letter, I feel I have been very optimistically inclined. We are really having a hard time, but God's grace is infinitely great. Betsie is often hungry. Nothing is coming in at the moment. Do send parcels again as soon as you can.

Be of good courage. God reigns.

Your Corrie

July 12

Dear All,

I am writing while at work. Your letter of June 6 was received. We are still under mail and parcel ban. We are doing well. Many of these women are so kind to us. There is a pleasant, hopeful air of uncertainty in camp. Do you suppose something is about to happen? I hope and believe that we shall be released by September 1, if peace has not come even before then. Then we shall have been in for six months; now if they only include Scheveningen, too, in their reckoning! Usually it is six months at Vught.

We sometimes hear shooting in the Bunkers at night. We know what that means. Then we pray for the bereaved relatives, and also for those who may be next in turn. The atmosphere is frequently very depressing. The men, especially, are having a hard time. Much has happened these last days. Men were called out of ranks during roll call and shot a few minutes later. We know that the dangers are very great in society at large also. This morning these lines came to me:

"Our hearts rejoice that God alone
Is seated still upon His throne."

Leny Franse and I walk together a little while each morning, and we speak almost exclusively of spiritual things. It gives me strength for the entire day. Leny is a heroine, and her husband a hero. They had lost everything and have made a conscious sacrifice of it. They are of the stuff of which martyrs are made. Not I; I long terribly for home, for luxury, for prosperity. That I have been able to hold my own is only by the grace of God. He supports me. I shall leave this place tempered and prepared for the time to come. To be a prisoner is terrible, though we are not always equally conscious of it. At six thirty in the morning we march away and work until six thirty in the evening. During that time we are much like free factory workers. Now and then we hear "thick clouds"; then we work steadily and stay in the groove. But on the whole there is an agreeable atmosphere. I work hard, but have pleasant work, the final inspection of relays for radios. It is painstaking, precise work, but much easier than repairing watches.

In the morning there is always a moment of intense suspense for everyone who may have any prospect of being released. First there is roll call for the barracks in which we sleep. That is the time scoldings are handed out, sometimes punishments or threats, all in the German manner. I always look

meanwhile at the beautiful Brabant skies. It is usually at sunrise or a bit
earlier, and we can see the whole expanse of sky from east to west. After roll
call we fall in for work crews, Betsie for the sewing room, and I for Philips.
Then comes the moment of suspense. Katja, the Aufseherin, *appears with*
a paper from the Kommandantur, *and reads off certain numbers. These*
step forward, knowing that they are either to be freed or to be überführt,
that is, transported into Germany. I always wonder, "Will my number be
among them? Suppose . . . Suppose. . . ?"

"In step. March. Left, two, three, four."

We march away, facing straight ahead as long as we are in sight of the
officers and Aufseherinnen. *A long day lies ahead of us. We were not among*
them; our numbers were not called. It never makes me unhappy. I am so
convinced that what the Lord wills is good. But I do long for release. Work is
a great diversion; the days and weeks fly past. Sundays are wonderful: work
forenoons, roll call at twelve, and then we are free. Betsie and I enjoy each
other's company so much. We prepare our "tea" as best we can, wash ourselves
well, sleep, and lie outside, and talk with our fellow believers. For some of
them I am too liberal, for others, too conservative; but God's Spirit gives a
blessing which works beyond, and perhaps even through, these differences.

What a long time six months of one's life is! But we are creatures of eternity;
for us it is but a short time.

Mrs. Boileu works in the same factory barracks with me. She is a splen-
did person, a real aristocrat. She has sacrificed everything. Her two sons
have been shot to death. Yet she is always sunny, and her conversation is
stimulating.

I must close. Keep courage!

Your Corrie

Recreation In Vught

Jantje was singing a ballad. He was our *laufer* or errand boy, the "printer's devil" of the entire Philips factory area. He was about sixteen. Lydia had been singing melodies of Grieg and Bach; they had sounded like home to me. Her voice was clear and bright, a bit thin without accompaniment but still lovely. Immediately afterwards came Jantje; he sang of a child whose father was a pilot who had died. It was mournful and sentimental.

Just then the radio screeched, after a few rattling coughs, "Errand boy wanted in Barracks 23. I repeat, Errand boy wanted in Barracks 23."

Jantje disappeared, and it was quiet in the barracks.

It was Sunday evening. Contests were being held. A path was marked off with strips of silvery paper which was used to brighten every small party. A child of three-and-a-half was crying pathetically. Her mother was somewhat strict in her views, and thought it worldly to look at such activities on Sunday. I tried to explain to her that she was planting a germ of dislike of the Sabbath, where love should be fostered. She let herself be persuaded; and the child looked on with face beaming as the girls ran a sack race, pushed each other along the path in wheelbarrows, and played many other amusing little games. There was much laughter, screaming and applause. The area resounded with it all.

Suddenly the gate flew open, and Katja, the *Aufseherin*, rushed in. She fretted and fumed, and announced an immediate *Blocksperre*, which meant that no one was to leave the barracks for the rest of the day. In addition, we were to be under mail, parcel and block restrictions for at least a month. In a twinkling the area was deserted and dead. Entering the dining room, I expected to hear a great deal of complaining, but there was not a bit of it. Everyone was sitting cheerfully, eating or talking, and no one seemed to take it seriously. The expressions on their faces seemed to say, "We've all had to bear so much, we can easily take this too." "We shall not let our courage lag; we'll hold our heads up high."

The restrictions did not materialize after all. The *Oberknol*[22] thought the *Aufseherin* had been too hasty and decided to wait until she herself found some reason for punishment.

"Lawsuit"

Jettie had kissed a Belgian. The men in the office next to our workroom were planning to teach her a lesson, and were now going to play courtroom. They had put on paper *dickies*[23] to simulate a judge's formal attire. Jettie was the defendant; she was accused, defended, and sentenced. It was all done with incredible realism, and was so very original and witty. But then, the "judges" were actually attorneys and other intellectuals; one was a professor, another a rector. We enjoyed anything that rose above the banalities of camp life. Jet had to take a good bit of ribbing. She was an attractive, glib child, who got along better with men than with women. She had gone through a lot. Most amusing of all was the judge, who dragged in theories of race hygiene and a lot of other national socialist nonsense. It was sparklingly witty and brought a college atmosphere into the factory surroundings.

"Fifteen!" The court scene broke up, paper dickies were torn off, and in no time everyone was at his desk or bench. When "Santa Claus" came in there was nothing to be seen. Fortunately, he had been momentarily detained by Mrs. Van der Zee, who complained of a headache. With great seriousness he pulled the aspirin out of his pocket, and a few minutes later, when he saw her running into the washroom because she could no longer restrain her laughter, he said to her, "You'd better sit down quietly now, or you'll have more headaches." Meanwhile, everything was again in order, and everyone was working as if nothing had happened. Had we turned into naughty schoolchildren?

As I write so about Vught, it all looks only relatively bad. Was this perhaps little more than a wartime adventure which, in the final analysis, would prove to have been an interesting experience? No, indeed; Vught was terrible. External circumstances did not appear unfavorable: the work was not too heavy; we got plenty of fresh air and sunshine; there was friendship and affection among the prisoners. What, then, made it so bad? Was it because I and others—women like my mother, for instance—were dealt with as army recruits?

Our freedom had been taken from us. One never realizes what that means until he has lived in imprisonment.

> *"How scornfully now are we beaten*
> *In captivity's fettering clamp.*
> *How waste we our days now in durance*
> *Imprisoned in barb-closured camp."*

The bad part of it lay not in the material situation but in the fact that it was forced upon us by those who were our enemies. There was a constant feeling of helplessness. We no longer had things under control. We forfeit many comforts when we go camping also, but we do so willingly.

Our fate was in the hands of stupid, inferior creatures. We knew that we were spied upon by Germans, and even by their satellites, which was worse. Fellow prisoners would at times play the traitor for an additional morsel of food. We never knew what might happen to us the next minute. We were actually and constantly surrounded by threats.

Contrasts

The atmosphere of this place can be understood only by those who have lived in it. I cannot describe it. Perhaps a snapshot or two would help; but no, they too would be inadequate, as photographs always are. Only a painter, an artist, could portray its mood, its spirit.

The record player was screeching. There were eight records that were played constantly—mournful music that only a few of us could appreciate, but it was played as loudly as possible by the few who enjoyed it.

Lily and I were sitting behind the soldering table discussing a sermon. She had such a sweet expression on her face; one could not look at her enough. We were speaking about "Forgetting the things which are behind . . . I press on toward the goal unto the prize of the high calling of God in Christ Jesus."

The machinery was noisy; everyone was talking; there was a jumble of sounds. Outside, the sun was shining on the white birches and on the electrified barbed wire. Suddenly there was a cracking and tearing sound—and the cardboard ceiling started to come down. A Belgian man and woman, newly engaged, had sought solitude up there and had fallen partway through. The foreman jumped up on the table and pushed up the broken pieces of paperboard, while another man hastily pounded a few nails into the thin laths which held it all together.

We came marching along, nicely in step. *Aufseherin* Hanny had just said, "Are you going to march as well as you did yesterday?"

"Oh, yes," we replied, "we'll do it for you; you are always so kind."

Sometimes she screamed at us as she stood in front of the troop; but that was prescribed, and her eyes were laughing at the same time. Her face always looked friendly under her jauntily cocked military cap. "Left, two, three, four."

We passed through the gate of the factory and on into the area in which we lived. I came to a halt right up in front, where the *Aufseherinnen* were standing together. Some of them were *Ehrenbrauten*,[24] common young girls reared under the regime. They had now been given authority over a large number, about seven hundred, of older, more refined, and better educated people. There were seven of them, headed by the *Oberknol*, a twisted soul with cruel eyes, twenty-two years of age. All of them wore gray uniforms. The *Ober* came up to Margie. "You've painted your lips; why do you do that, to please the men, or perhaps me? You women are idiots; you run around in dark overalls with numbers on them and still want to use makeup."

She pulled the kerchief off another. Aha! Curls! They were forbidden; the hair should be tied up in a band. "Don't forget you are prisoners."

Marie denied having made herself up. She was a young woman with long eyelashes, a dreamy young face, and blond hair. Last year she saw her husband murdered before her eyes; since then she had been a prisoner here, already for more than a year.

The skies of Brabant were a blue dome over our heads, with brightly colored and golden clouds, and soft pastels along the horizon. A heron was flying above us.

Katja, the youngest *Aufseherin*, walked past the troop. She was expecting a child. Camp gossip said that the father was Meyerhof, a very tall officer who had been for a time our head man. He was a cruel person, who raged and scolded terribly. Katja always looked at us with great animosity. She had the power to injure us and used it whenever she could. She scolded and raved like a child of the streets, and threatened us with the most impossible punishments. Yet, as I looked at her, I could see that she was really a wretchedly unhappy child. She was about nineteen or twenty years of age, and the corners of her mouth were turned down in a perpetual pout.

Standing in ranks beside us were the children, about twenty of them, large and small, the youngest a sweet little fellow in the arms of his mother. He suddenly called out, "Katte ja" and put out his pudgy hands to Katja. How natural that seemed! Our standing at attention was unnatural. The child, with his dimpled cheeks, still knew nothing of coercion. Katja's face changed instantly. She said something like "dear little fellow" and caressed him as she passed by.

Children in imprisonment are the greatest comfort and, at the same time, the saddest thing one can imagine. Here in Vught they looked wonderfully healthy. In the cells at Scheveningen a child's voice could drive one to despair. They were never given any fresh air, and were permitted only rarely to run up and down the corridor.

"Is the door going to stay open now?" I once heard a very tiny fellow ask his mother in a low voice. That was imprisonment!

This morning Number 1 was called out. She had been here longer than any of us. Even the *Aufseherin*, who had brought the list from the commander and who had apparently not yet looked at the numbers, expressed some pleasure. "Oh, just listen, Number 1!"

Out she came, from the ranks, where the work commandos were standing five abreast. She tottered when she reached the front of the office, and we called out to her, "Sit down!" She collapsed on the uncomfortable birch-log bench, and sat with her head down on her arms on the back of the bench. She was still sitting that way as we marched off. "In step, march! Left, two, three, four." The clouds in the east were so beautifully colored they cast a glow upon us.

The Round Red Patch

In the sewing room Betsie saw that one of the women was sewing a large round patch on a square of white cloth and sewing this in turn on the back of a blue overall. It was for Mrs. Bosman, who had tried to escape from the "Bosch," a camp not far from here, and who had been captured with two others. It no doubt would mean the bunker for her; and as long as she wore her overall, she was also to wear the round red patch as a "badge of honor." She had climbed over several roofs and run far away, but had been captured and brought back. She was kept standing for hours. She was not permitted to go to bed, but made to sit all night on the floor of the soldiers' dormitory. She looked tired, but was as cheerful and brave as always. She had just received word that her husband, Dr. Bosman, had been wounded by grenade fragments as he was riding on a train. He was said to have lost several fingers, but was otherwise all right.

I recalled the last time I had seen Mr. Bosman in Haarlem, and felt proud of the women of Holland.

The "Red-Light Commandos"

Good-looking but ignorant faces, clamorous voices; you always knew when they were around. They were entirely without fear. When everyone else was listening in deathlike silence to the scolding of our "superior," they would boldly call out a reply; and if the superiors happened to be men, they knew it would not get them into trouble. They were always the last to appear at roll call. There were always a few of them standing along the barbed wire fence that separated us from the men's section, and sometimes they would climb up on to the window frames to look out over the men's area. We were warned at roll call to report all those we saw there.

"You're certainly not all whores!" screamed the *Aufseherin*.

Janneke

It was warm in the barracks. The spools of the relays were sticking as if they were about to melt. The fire brigade was sprinkling the roof. I wondered if they were just practicing, or if they thought the sun would burn less hotly on the tarred roof. Now and then a drop of melted tar fell into the gutter along the windows. Some of the women were sleeping in the most uncomfortable positions, one on a bench with her head on packing material, most of them lying forward with their heads on their arms. Outside, the air shimmered above the baking earth. I had nothing on but my overalls, and had the legs rolled up high.

The door flew open. Jan was pursuing Janneke. Both carried large mugs of water and threw it at each other over the workbenches, without giving a thought to the valuable tools and radio parts lying there. It became a rough-and-tumble affair. Janneke was a large Belgian woman with laughing eyes. Jan was our foreman, a communist. The floor was soaking wet. Finally, Janneke was carried, with much applause, by Jan and the others to the washroom, where they threw her into a washtub and turned on the water.

"Thick clouds," cried someone.

In an instant, everyone was quietly at work, the laughter died down, and we were all apparently very industrious. Janneke had flown into the toilet room, and the cleaning woman was mopping the floor, when the much-feared Muller walked in. Everything was so "correct" that there was nothing to scold about and nothing to report. Muller's eyes seemed to bristle more than ever.

It was morning. The supply cart was wheeled in, a low wagon with small, rattling iron wheels. The room was filled with noise, for the cart was intentionally bumped against everything to increase the clatter. Janneke jumped onto the cart and was given a wild and noisy ride through the room. Screams, laughter, thumping! Wildly excited, and all out of breath, Janneke rolled off the cart and was tossed onto the table as the finale to the roughhousing. Janneke was large and fat.

The radio was blaring "Everything Passes On."

We were standing outside the office. It was evening, and it had been a long day. Though we hadn't actually worked eleven hours, we had been in the factory that long. And we never got enough sleep. One grew so very tired in Vught, and in the evening longed so for rest in bed. But now we had to stand at attention outside the office until we were ordered to enter and hear our sentence. All ten of us had been reported. A short distance away stood a group of newcomers waiting to be given their uniforms. They stood and talked carelessly, while we stood at attention. Those who were subject to punishment for any misdemeanor became the butt of every criticism one could think of. We talked in undertones about the possibilities. It would very likely be "the bunker." Janneke and I were guilty of the same offense. While washing our hands we had talked to the new cleaning man. We talked about his work at home; he was a small farmer from North Holland. As he told me how he had always rented the dike for grazing his four cows, the *Aufseherin* stood suddenly behind us. All my muscles had tensed for a minute from shock; and then, she took down our numbers, birthdates, a complete *procès-verbal*.

"You may not talk with the men; it is forbidden."

Janneke said: "If it should be the bunker, I hope we can stay together. Listen, shall we spend a lot of time praying? So little comes of it here. How quiet it will be! I'll hide my rosary under my clothing."

It turned out to be not as bad as we had expected; nothing more than a warning, typed on heavy, impressive paper. It was signed, however, and filed in a dossier. Janneke, too, got off in the same way. Meyerhof made it a point to scold some women, but for Janneke he always had a smile. Janneke had two rows of even white teeth.

During an air raid Janneke was struck in the hip by a shell fragment and was taken to the hospital. But I knew she had her rosary with her!

Play of Colors

It was Sunday afternoon. We were already walking outside. The weather was beautiful, and miracles were taking place above and around us. There were hints of freedom coming soon.

Colors appeared in the sky—rainbow colors—not in a fixed bow opposite the sun but here and there in arcs of a circle, irrespective of the position of the sun. There was a rippling play of light on one of the clouds which apparently was the reflection from some surface of water. How I wish I were a Felix Timmermans to be able to describe it. We called everyone outside. What a display of colors! What a marvel of nature! I had never seen anything like it. The Lord was writing a message, a heavenly message, across the skies.

Did it mean that there would again be color in our lives, that freedom was at hand, and the end had come of somber wartime sorrow? Or did the Lord want to direct the eyes of our souls upward, saying, "Look up unto Me. In Me there is light, and beauty, and joy of colors. Do not fix your gaze on your present circumstances which are difficult and grievous; lift up your eyes and your hearts on high!"

Was God permitting us to see a bit of heaven?

"Oh, Betsie, look; the colors are changing; and gold is added. Oh, Betsie, it is a bit of heaven!"

"Where Father is experiencing fullness of joy," whispered Betsie. "And some day we, too, shall be allowed to share it with him." What happiness colors can bring!

Freedom Beckons

It was now August of 1944. Allied forces had landed in Normandy on June the sixth. It was rumored that the Princess Irene Brigade was in France and approaching Belgium. The Brigade was part of the Dutch forces that had escaped to England during the Five-Day War; now it was marching to reclaim its own. We speculated, as if it were a matter of centimeters, how far they were from Vught!

Everyone talked to everyone else. We were only mildly interested in work. If it was poorly done, well, what of it? If we did not reach our quota . . . there were more important things.

Those with low numbers did not dare to be happy. In concentration camps people were numbered as they entered. Low numbers thus indicated people who had been in prison a long time. "Hope deferred maketh the heart sick" (Prov. 13:12), and they had hoped for so long. Some had been here a year and a half, but now they talked in terms of weeks. The *Aufseherinnen* were low-spirited that morning. "Thick clouds" or "Fifteen" were not so much as heard. At the gate of Philips stood not a single officer. "Santa Claus" was playing the hypocrite with Liesel. He was "so sorry" for us, "such cultured women," and the *Aufseherinnen* were such hussies, and there we were, at their mercy! Of him we need never be afraid, he suffered with us.

Santa Claus was so named because he had come into the camp at Christmas time and had beaten two men to death the day of his arrival.

"So you gauge them at twelve milliamperes," said the spot-checker to me. But my thoughts were in Haarlem and in Belgium. How much longer? I was much more interested in how many kilometers the Princess Irene Brigade was from Holland than in those stupid milliamperes.

A boy stood talking happily with a group of girls about him.

"It is a matter of four days, at most," said he. "It is the twenty-fourth of August today, and you'll see; when we wake up in the morning all the guards will have disappeared."

Between twelve and one I was lying on "the sands" with Mien, letting my fancies roam. Mien had no imagination. I was saying to her:

"We are walking in the Zijlstraat. Do you see the light from the west shining on the Grote Kerk? There are more than a hundred shades of gray. Now we are entering the church; I hear the organ playing. Marie Barbas, the organist, knows we are there and plays: 'When You Are Sore in Need' and 'Whatever the Future May Bring.'

"How beautifully the sun shines through the stained-glass windows! Do you smell the damp, musty air? Dominee Van der Waal is climbing into the pulpit. . . ."

"The guard is being changed," said Mien.

I sighed and looked at the picturesque guardhouse, where a cover had been drawn over the machine guns.

"Mien, I have just met you in the Grote-Houtsstraat.[25] Won't you go with me to Vroom en Dreesman and have a *thé-complet*?"

"What is that?" asked Mien.

"A whole pot of tea, enough for at least three or four cups, and a petit four, and cakes, and bonbons, and a savory bit."

"We're having pea soup with barley today," said Mien.

"But you are not in Vught; you are in Haarlem," I insisted, but I did not succeed in drawing her away from present realities.

Everyone was happy in Barracks 35. People were sitting cheerfully at work. There was much talking. Those who entered walked over in a quasi-casual manner to their friends, and whispered the latest news. There was an atmosphere of hope in the room.

In the washroom of Barracks 24 lay a package of bread, prepared that morning by Mrs. Diederiks to give to her husband, who worked in the same barracks with her. She was a gentle woman with an uncommonly fine, intelligent face. Under her heart she was carrying her first child.

During the night Mr. Diederiks had been executed by a firing squad.

Suspense

Bridges were being blown up in the vicinity. The explosions were so great that we kept our mouths open to protect our eardrums.

Now there was anxiety in our hearts instead of happy anticipation. Near the barbed wire fence which separated us from the men's camp the women were clambering up on benches and window frames. Something was happening over there: all of the men were standing in ranks on the great square.

A pale-faced little woman said to me: "I can see my husband standing there from here. Do you suppose this will be the last time? I am so afraid they are going to do something awful to him."

There was silence until someone said, "Now men are being called forward out of the various groups." We heard names being called out, but could not distinguish them. We waited. A great terror had seized upon us all.

"Now they are marching out of the gate. Oh, they are certainly being transported to Germany."

The sound of many marching feet was heard for several minutes, and then gradually died away. It was deathly quiet. We were waiting. For what? Then one woman jumped down from a bench and disappeared into the barracks, and gradually the rest followed. It was unpleasantly quiet. No one said a word.

And then we heard one hundred and eighty shots.

Every shot meant the death of a good Netherlander. That we knew. I laid my head on Betsie's shoulder. Could misery become so great that one would collapse under it?

"Betsie, I cannot bear it. Why, O Lord, why dost Thou permit this to happen?"

Didn't Betsie know what was happening? Her face looked so serene, almost happy. Had God put a hedge about her, as He did about Job? Had this dreadful thing not penetrated her being? I took her hand and led her gently to the other side of the barracks, away from the inexpressible grief of all these women who did not know whether one of those hundred and eighty bullets had struck her husband, her fiancé, or her son. We sat down on one of the rough birch-log benches.

I spoke now to the Lord. "Thou hast borne all our griefs, O Lord. Wilt Thou not also bear this one?"

"Yes, My child, and you yourself need not, and cannot, and may not bear the sorrows of the world about you."

"But, Lord, I have seen and heard this thing, and it was so very horrible! Oh Lord, why, why?"

"I look down upon the trouble and grief of man with the intent that it shall be surrendered unto Me. Cast all your burdens upon Me."

"O Lord, give me then Thy Holy Spirit, that I may bring this great sorrow to Thee and leave it with Thee."

And then I became calm within. I recalled suddenly a quiet Sunday evening in Lunteren years ago. The Sadhu Sundhar Singh sat before us, and we might ask him any question we wished. A young student asked, "Why did God permit so many innocent people to die in the war?"

The Sadhu answered, "Because God thought it necessary for them."

I went with Betsie to the barracks, and a bit later was lying beside her in bed. I did not sleep, but rested quietly—and there was peace in my heart. God makes no mistakes. Everything looks like a confused piece of embroidery work, meaningless and ugly. But that is the underside. Some day we shall see the right side and shall be amazed and thankful.

Transport to Germany

"Betsie, we are in a difficult class in the school of life, but Jesus is standing in front of the class. He Himself is teaching us; some day we shall take the final examination; and if we willingly accept His teaching, we shall be successful. The next class will not be so difficult."

"We shall soon have vacation," said Betsie.

It was the fourth of September. We were sitting on our heels in a boxcar. There was room for forty people in it; but there were eighty of us. We still managed to assume a sitting position. There was not a window in the place, only a couple of narrow, grilled ventilators, which let in very little air. The stench was dreadful, and I felt sick. As we were forming in ranks beside the transport I had suddenly felt ill. We were kept standing for hours, and saw on every hand how Vught was being emptied. Carts full of dossiers had gone to the ovens, and a bit later we saw the smoke rising. The sick from the *Revier*[26] passed us in large vehicles; among them were emaciated bodies and deathly sick men. All of them were carried into the long train.

Where were we going?

We already knew that this did not mean freedom. Gradually that thought had penetrated into our minds, and hope had fled to make way for despairing certainty—transported to Germany! Away from our Netherlands, where freedom would soon reign. Deep into evil Germany—insecure, subject to the whims of cruel enemies, who could do with us as they willed. I had a feeling of suffocation. Round about us sat the Red-light Commandos. They were rough girls and women; now they were frustrated, fearful and furious. Their lewd language made our confinement in the boxcar still more horrible. But they, too, were on the verge of smothering from lack of oxygen. With a knife and other hard objects, some were trying to pry holes in the walls. The wood was hard, but old and weathered, and they succeeded in breaking through.

They worked steadily at enlarging the air holes, and gradually the feeling of suffocation passed and we felt a wonderful draught of fresh air. At least we would not stifle!

Leaning tightly against me was an *Ehrenbraut*. She had been seized because she had infected a German soldier. She was friendly to me, and changed her position a bit to give my legs a little more room. I spoke softly with her for, in the storm of life, we had been brought side by side. I thought about her future, and spoke to her of the Lord Jesus who could make her happy.

"If you ever need my help, will you come to me? I live. . ." But where did I live? Would the Barteljorisstraat ever again be my home? I was going into an uncertain future.

> *It matters not what the morrow may bring,*
> *For my Savior is holding my hand.*
> *With courage from Him, I will lift up my eyes,*
> *And face toward the strange distant land.*
> *Oh, teach me to follow, no question to ask,*
> *Whatever Thou doest is good.*
> *Oh, teach me to carry but one day's task*
> *With courage and calmness of mood.*

How often I had sung those lines, and how easily!

Now every word was pregnant with meaning, but also with comfort.

Suddenly there was a clatter of hailstones on the roof of the car. Hailstones? Why, of course not, they were bullets. With a jolt the train came to a stop. The machine gun on the roof of our car was no doubt the target. A sharp patter against the sides of the car made us shrink together. A salvo of shots followed, but the walls held. In breathless suspense we huddled together. I gripped Betsie's hand. We were both calm. Did this mean rescue or death? We were still on this side of the border with Germany; but if the attempt did succeed, where could we go? There were thousands of prisoners on the train. It proved, indeed, to be an attempt at rescue, but it had not been sufficiently well planned. Two of the rescuers were seized. It was awful to contemplate what would happen to them. The rest managed to escape. The train remained at a standstill for a long time, and then proceeded across the border. In a car up ahead someone was singing,

Adieu beloved Netherlands
"Dear fatherland, farewell."

Many of us would never see our homeland again. What sadness there was in that song! I had heard it before at the sailing of a boat to India. Then, too, there had been a note of sadness in it; there, too, people were weeping, because of the long, perhaps final, separation from loved ones. And yet that journey was a voluntary one, and led to a consciously selected goal.

Gradually it grew dark. I fell asleep and forgot my surroundings. The train carried us ever farther into Germany. When I awakened it was already light in the car, and bread and butter were being distributed. There was a large quantity of bread. Some of the women had piled up the loaves to make seats for themselves. I wondered if the amount of bread indicated a long journey. It was horrible to travel under such conditions. The filth was indescribable. No provision had been made for our most elemental needs. I felt increasingly ill and gradually sank into an apathy which made me indifferent to all about me. Betsie was looking through a crevice in the wall, and reported what she saw of poor Germany—ruined towns, but also lovely rolling fields and woods, such as we used to enjoy on vacation trips abroad. Parts of the country looked so peaceful.

Farther and deeper into Germany we went. Three long days and three still longer nights, and finally we arrived at Oranienburg, just north of Berlin. There the larger section of the train, carrying the men, was uncoupled.

I begged for water. Now and then a bucketful was shoved in, but there was no cooperation in our car; whoever was closest to it snatched it away from the others. What a torment thirst can be! One of the women now pounded on the door and cried, "There is a sick woman here who will die of thirst if you don't bring some water."

The doors slid open. How delicious that fresh air was! I breathed deeply. But the women surged into the open doors to enjoy the air and to look outside. And it again became stifling. Betsie held a mug of water to my lips. What a relief! I drank and drank, and it took great effort to save some for later on when that awful thirst would return. But then I fell into a stupor and imagined I was elsewhere, in a hospital ward. I tried to call out, "Nurse, please give me some water," but I could not.

When next I came to, the train was standing still in Fürstenberg. The sliding doors opened wide, and we staggered outside. How wonderful! Our spirits rose instantly and we became almost cheerful. Friends found one another again. After much delay we marched five abreast to camp Ravensbruck. We were allowed to go slowly. Villagers passed us, and I debated whether I dared ask one of them for a drink, for I was again being tormented by thirst. It was a question, also, whether they would be allowed to give it to me. Were they permitted to speak to prisoners? Would they want to? They were Germans. And we? We were despised Dutch prisoners.

Soldiers were walking behind us; only a few, however. What could we do, anyway? It takes only a few soldiers to guard weak, weary and travel-worn women. We halted near a lake and I could go no farther. Betsie and a friend had been supporting me; now I collapsed on the grass and gazed about me. I saw a beautiful lake and, beyond, its spire rising white against the hills, a little church and abbey. I saw woods and fields. How lovely the world was meant to be, and what a sorry place man has made of it! The landscape brought to my mind the words of the twenty-third psalm: ". . . green pastures . . . beside the still waters." My mind went on, "Yea, though I walk through the valley of the shadow of death, I will fear no evil, Thy rod and thy staff they comfort me."

The Valley of the Shadows

A great gate led into the camp of Ravensbruck, situated about forty miles north of Berlin. The gate opened, and we marched in past the guards. On both sides stood S.S. officers and *Aufseherinnen*. We marched five abreast. We were wearing our Vught uniforms of blue overalls; and there was strength in the bearing of these women about me. One of them started singing:

> *We never let our courage lag;*
> *We hold our heads up high;*
> *Never shall they get us down,*
> *Though they be ever so sly.*
> *O yea! O yea! you Netherlands women,*
> *Heads up, heads up, heads up!*

Amazing to sing that ditty at such a moment as this! It looked appallingly as if they had got us down. Or was there an inner strength they could never defeat?

Hollanders who had already been in the camp for years said to us later, "We were proud of you as you came marching in; you were so brave and spirited." Even the commander was said to have remarked, "I don't understand these Hollanders. You pack them into boxcars for three days, and then they came marching into my camp with heads up as if to say, 'It doesn't hurt me at all; you'll never get me down.' And the first thing they all do is go to a tap to wash themselves."

Indeed, our bearing was spirited and proud at the moment. But what would Ravensbruck do to us? Was pride enough, or would we need more than that to keep our heads up in this pool of misery and cruelty? As we stood on the *Lagerstrasse* we saw a work commando marching by. What sturdy, healthy-looking young girls there were in the group! "Is Ravensbruck going to be bearable, after all?" I asked myself. "It does look as if one could remain alive here." I still did not know that, though many young and strong people could endure the punishment, many weak and older ones died very quickly, and that even some strong ones did not survive the difficult and hazardous existence. But that is not entirely accurate either, for some weak and sick individuals did survive; they were, however, in the minority.

After standing a long time we were finally led to a large, carelessly erected tent, with a floor of straw that was swarming with lice and fleas. As we passed the barracks along the way, emaciated women begged for food; everywhere, skeletonlike hands reached out to us. We still had some food with us, and tried to throw them some bread. But the *Aufseherinnen* beat them away. What a place of hunger and cruelty! Through a window I talked to a Hollander. "What is it like here? Is it at all bearable?" And she gave me a cynical description of the life here. It made me unhappy and even angry. It could not be *that* bad; why should she try to discourage us? I refused to accept her story.

The tent was a bedlam. Betsie and I found a small space along the side and sat down on our blanket. When I saw all the vermin, I agreed with Betsie that we should cut our hair short. But as I cut her lovely, wavy hair, and then buried it in the sand, I was very unhappy. How foolish, really; there was so much that was infinitely worse. We were soon driven out of the tent and made to stand in line on the sand. The ground here was graded upward against the concrete wall which enclosed the camp on all sides. All along the wall were lines of barbed wire, carrying an electric current. Here and there a placard with skull and crossbones warned us of danger and formed a lugubrious decoration for the gray wall.

As evening fell, some of the women lay down on the ground. Betsie and I remained standing; but then it suddenly dawned on us that we were to spend the night here. We were to sleep out under the open sky. We lay down close together and drew our blanket over us. "He giveth His beloved sleep," said Betsie. I looked up at the stars above us. He who held the stars in their orbits would not leave us alone. "The night is dark, and I am far from home, lead Thou me on." And then we fell asleep.

I awakened when it began to rain, and pulled the blanket over our faces. It was midnight. What a pity that everything would now be wet! I glanced around. There were hundreds of people lying uncovered on the ground. All about and beyond us stood the black silhouettes of darkened barracks. What lay ahead of us in this concentration camp?

The crematorium, Ravensbruck.

4

The Horrors of Ravensbruck

Angels Round About Us

We were standing on the great open square in front of the administration building. Again it was night. We had thrown our arms around each other and drawn more closely about us the blanket we had carried with us from Vught. It was very cold. We had already spent two days and nights outside. Now we were standing in a long line, waiting in front of the bathhouse. At the door of the somber, dark building was a pile of clothing, packages, suitcases, provisions and blankets, all thrown together in a colorful, chaotic heap. Gradually it became a mountain. All possessions of the *Neue Zugaenge* (the new arrivals) were being taken from them.

There lay the precious treasures. Just imagine, for a minute, how much the fragments left from a Red Cross parcel meant to a hungry prisoner. Seeing this, we quickly ate whatever we had left. More serious was the sacrifice of our clothing. The women coming out of the shower room had on a thin dress, an undershirt, and a pair of wooden shoes—nothing more. A young woman beside me said, "This is worse than when they took everything out of my home." She told me about her pretty villa with its rose garden, her grand piano, and so many other precious things. "There is nothing left; everything has been taken. But this is much worse. Pretty soon we shall have no blanket and no clothing, nothing but a shirt and a dress."

I felt Betsie shivering and pressed her closely to me. "O Lord, save us from this evil; Betsie is so frail," I pleaded.

The night was dark; and I saw how many other weak, frail women, even aged ones, walked past me shivering as they came back from the wicked building, deprived of everything that had kept them warm.

"Betsie, are you prepared to offer this sacrifice also if God should ask it?"

"Corrie, I cannot do it," she whispered softly.

Oh, I could scarcely do it myself; but I was not thinking of myself then; I was suffering deeply with Betsie. Why did the Lord ask anything so hard from us? I pleaded, "O Lord, if Thou dost nevertheless ask this sacrifice of us, give us the strength to offer it; give us the willingness to make it."

A white silk shirt lay on top of the mountain of material beside the door. I watched as a gust of wind lifted it up and let it drop, one sleeve falling into a jar of apple butter.

An old woman stood quietly weeping.

An officer appeared in the doorway and screamed at us hoarsely, "Do you have any objections to surrendering your clothes? We'll soon teach you Hollanders what Ravensbruck is like." The light shone on his cruel face.

I put my arm around Betsie and led her into a dark corner. We had both heard our names being called and relayed sympathetically down the line: "ten Boom, Elizabeth; ten Boom, Cornelia."

"I cannot," repeated Betsie.

For a few minutes we were quiet and spoke softly with the Savior. He was with us and knew what we were suffering, and He loved us.

"Lord, if Thou dost ask this sacrifice of us, give us the strength to make it."

"Corrie, I am ready," whispered Betsie, softly.

"Then everything is all right," I answered.

I took her arm, and together we entered the terrifying building. At a table were women who took away all our possessions. Everyone had to undress completely and then go to a room where her hair was checked. If anyone had lice, her hair was clipped short. A sweet Belgian girl with beautiful golden hair was clipped at once. She had no lice; but, as we had observed, beautiful hair was invariably cut as a matter of principle. Steal or despoil everything you can seemed to be their slogan.

I asked a woman who was busy checking the possessions of the new arrivals if I might use the toilet. She pointed to a door, and I discovered that that convenience was nothing more than a hole in the shower-room floor. Betsie stayed close beside me all the time. Suddenly I had an inspiration. "Quick, take off your woolen underwear," I whispered to her. I rolled it up with mine and laid the bundle in a corner with my little Bible. The spot was alive with cockroaches, but I didn't worry about that. I felt wonderfully relieved and happy. "The Lord is busy answering our prayers, Betsie," I whispered, "we shall not have to make the sacrifice of all our clothes."

We hurried back to the row of women waiting to be undressed. A little later, after we had had our showers and put on our shirts and shabby dresses, I hid the roll of underwear and my Bible under my dress. It did bulge out obviously through my dress; but I prayed, "Lord, cause now Thine angels to surround me; and let them not be transparent today, for the guards must not see me." I felt perfectly at ease. Calmly I passed the guards. Everyone was checked, from the front, the sides, the back. Not a bulge escaped the eyes of the guard. The woman just in front of me had hidden a woolen vest under her dress; it was taken from her. They let me pass, for they did not see me. Betsie, right behind me, was searched.

But outside awaited another danger. On each side of the door were women who looked everyone over for a second time. They felt over the body of each one who passed. I knew that they would not see me, for the angels were still surrounding me. I was not even surprised when they passed me by; but within me rose the jubilant cry, "O Lord, if Thou dost so answer prayer, I can face even Ravensbruck unafraid."

The Quarantine Barracks

It was now very cold outside. We had to walk a short distance to Barracks 8, where we were to be quarantined, our first quarters in the camp. Once there, we quickly put on our woolen underwear. The miracle had taken place. We had been allowed to keep our Bible and our underwear. "They that trust in the Lord shall not be put to shame."

The rest of the Hollanders, too, were not left without underwear for long. Those who had long been in the camp managed gradually to "acquire" something for each one. One of the moral vexations in the camp proved to be that everyone was suspected of stealing the things she needed. We were happy to see that Hollanders gave away the things they acquired for us. It was beneath their dignity to bargain, as did especially the Polish women. Their legal tender was our meager daily portion of bread. A Polish woman would ask three portions of bread for a shirt, which meant that the purchaser had to live for three days on her ration of turnip soup and a couple of potatoes.

The quarantine barracks consisted of two large and two smaller rooms, in which a vast number of beds had been built in tiers of three. They stood close together, and from five to seven women were given two beds. I measured them with my hand. I had often practiced hand measuring with my club girls, and so I determined that each one of these beds was only 70 centimeters

Dreaded and dreadful Ravensbruck!

wide (27.5 inches). Five of us tried to lie lengthwise, but the straw sack mattress sloped down so on the sides that those on the outside kept falling off. Then we tried lying crosswise. We slept so close together that when one wanted to turn around, all five had to do so. There was very little ventilation. The next day we observed that hardly a ray of daylight reached our beds, for we happened to be in the center of the large room, too far from the windows.

Roll call now became by far the worst of the day's vexing occurrences. We were compelled to stand at attention for hours in the area between two of the barracks. No work had yet been assigned to us and, between roll calls, we usually sat idly on our dark beds. Very soon, however, we began to use our free time to talk to those in need of comfort. There were many of them. We had a small Bible and very cautiously read aloud from it.

We now came to know many individuals with whom we had at first had no contact. There was a friendly spirit among us.

After having spent two days in the open we were thankful to have at least a roof over our heads. We were also given blankets, three for the five of us. We did not suffer from the cold as long as we were inside.

One morning I was sitting on my bed looking around. Through the rows of beds I could see Betsie, sitting on a stool next to the window, mending. There was something homelike about the way she sat there. Her face was so peaceful and sweet. I sat looking at her. We were already adjusting ourselves to this strange life. The pleasant atmosphere which Betsie always seemed to create about her at home had not left her even here. Precisely and neatly she mended our garments with needle and thread borrowed from a friend. God had called us to this place, and here was now our task. I had to learn not to look forward constantly to being released but to accept the fact that I was here and that my calling was here.

Through the window climbed Tine Delarive. She was seriously ill with tuberculosis, and was in the hospital barracks with all the rest who had been ill when we left Vught. I was always so glad to see her; she was such a brave woman.

"Have you run away from the hospital?" I asked her.

"Things are simply unbearable over there," said she. "It has already happened three times that one of my bedfellows has died in the evening, and I have had to lie abed all night beside a corpse. They do not remove the bodies until morning."

Higher Appeal

Worn out from standing during roll call, for which everyone had to appear at 4:30 in the morning, we were again lying on our beds. The beds above us were so low that we could not sit upright, and bits of straw and filth sifted down upon us. The five of us lay tightly pressed together, but we were thankful to be allowed to rest. Then someone shouted, "All out for roll call!"

Again? Listlessly we walked outside. I looked around, and an *Aufseherin* gave me a nasty blow on my neck. The cruel intent hurt even more than the blow, which I felt for some time.

"*Schneller, aber schneller!*"[27] she screamed in a hoarse voice.

We were kept standing for another hour. Our endurance was about at an end. A cart approached with our food; but if any of us thought we would be permitted to go inside before eating we were to be disappointed. We had to eat outside, and those who tried to enter the barracks encountered the *Blockalteste*,[28] who kept them out.

So it went the whole day long. We were no more than settled inside when someone would cry: "Fall in, Roll call!"

"This cannot go on," said someone. "One of us must try to get through to the *Lagerführer*[29] to report how we are being treated."

Someone asked Betsie's advice.

"No," said she, "that would do no good. We must appeal higher up and ask the *Weltführer*.[30] He, the Lord, alone can help us."

Later we learned that these ordeals had been deliberately planned to tire us, to break our spirits, and to weaken our morale. It was fortunate that no one had gone to the *Lagerführer*, for he was an unspeakably cruel man. The *Weltführer* is always accessible, and He not only helps us to bear our burdens but He bears us also.

Parade in the Nude

We were lined up in the hospital corridor for medical inspection. We had to remove all our clothes and lay them on the floor of the entrance hall. When I pulled my coat on over my naked body, someone snarled at me. It looked as if I were trying to evade something.

"Of course, we understand what you're trying to do; run along, throw away that coat and stand in line."

Shivering from cold and misery, I tried to distract my attention from my own discomfort by looking at those around me, with as much interest as I could muster—much as one will pinch his thumbs when in great pain. But it was of no use. Never in my life had I felt so wretched, so cold, or so humiliated. It *always* seemed at the moment that the present ordeal was the worst I had yet experienced, but this one certainly was worse than any that had preceded it.

Suddenly I recalled a painting of Jesus on Golgotha. For the first time I realized that Jesus had hung naked upon the cross. How He must have suffered! He, God's Son, whose home was heaven! And all that suffering He bore for me, that I might someday go to heaven.

O Jesus, can the pain I bear
Compare with what You bore for me?
And can I not in my despair
Find courage as I look on Thee?

Was it for me You bore the Cross
To set me free and cleanse from stain?
And shall I murmur at my loss
When Thou art here, my lasting gain?

My soul became calm within me. I felt that strength was given me to go on. I prayed, "O Savior, Thou didst once suffer for me on Calvary. I thank Thee for it. Help me now to bear this present experience. Give me strength!"

"The sufferings of this present time are not worthy to be compared with the glory which shall be revealed."

Betsie and I stood hand in hand. It was a long time that day before the doctor arrived. He was a tall man in uniform. He sat on the edge of a table and had us march past him. He himself did nothing but look at us. A woman dentist examined our teeth; one woman doctor looked at our throat, another, between our fingers. Stripping was not at all necessary for the examination; it was intended solely to humiliate and distress us.

The sufferings of Jesus became very real to me because of all these experiences. Among the most terrifying things here were the sounds we heard—the swishing of the lash, the screams of its victims, the hoarse, screeching voices, and the yelling and snarling of cruel, wicked people; it all made a hell out of Ravensbruck. Jesus, too, must have heard such sounds—He whose ears were attuned to the music of heaven. How great must have been His love for us to have endured so much for our salvation!

Mentally Deficient

We had a half hour of leisure and were walking past one of the barracks. Through a window I could look into a small concrete-walled room. There stood a feebleminded child, barefoot, and with no clothing on except a short vest. She was horribly emaciated, almost a skeleton, and stood leaning against the cold wall. There was a vacant look in her eyes.

"Can you understand how human life can be so tenacious?" said someone to me. "That child has been living here for weeks on half rations; she sleeps at night on the concrete floor, without mattress or blanket; and she can still stand upright."

I turned away. Was this thing I was seeing a reality? It seemed more like a bad dream.

"O Lord," I prayed, "please let me be released soon, so that I may establish a home for other feebleminded people, where they may have much love, much care, and good nursing. Lord, take this poor child unto Thyself quickly. And save us; save the world from this terrible regime."

I did not understand the "why" of suffering except that of my own suffering in this place. God had brought me here for a specific task. I was here to lead the sorrowing and the despairing to the Savior. I was to see how He comforted them. I was to point the way to heaven to people among whom were many that would soon be dying. Others would continue to live, but henceforth as happy children of God because they had come to know Jesus who gives them heavenly joy and peace and comfort for their lives and for the hour of death. As far as I myself was concerned, I had here received the blessing of a better understanding of the suffering of the Lord Jesus, and consequently a deeper appreciation of His great love. I was learning under all circumstances not to rely on my own strength, but as a child to talk over everything with Him who is in all things the conqueror. I saw more clearly my own insignificance and His greatness, and felt myself purified and growing stronger. The "why" of my own suffering was no problem to me. But all the other suffering, which was so much worse! I knew that Ravensbruck was only one of very many concentration camps, and that there was limitless suffering in the bombarded cities, on the battlefields, and in the occupied countries. I knew that judgments were in the earth more terrible than ever before in human history.

The martyred, weak-minded child I saw was a representative of the suffering of the great masses I did not see; but the suffering of all of them was just as real to me as was that of the dying woman coming toward me. She was being carried in an old blanket held at the four corners by thin fellow prisoners. Her skeletonlike legs dangled helplessly over the edge. There were so many sick and dying that there had not been enough stretchers available that morning.

In a corner of the room where there was light enough for me to read, I turned to the Revelation of Saint John. It is such a wonderful book. It is of such great importance that judgment is declared on anyone who adds to or takes away from it, and a blessing is pronounced on those who read and keep its words.

I did not know if the things about which I read were now happening, if the symbolical but terrible events referred to the present or to the future. But this I did understand, and this gave me something to hold onto: these world judgments were included in God's plan. All of this was not just a mistake; God makes no mistakes. He looks upon trouble and grief with the intent that we shall bring it to Him and leave it with Him. That was the lesson I had to learn here.

This, too, I had learned: that I was not called upon to bear the grief and the cares of the whole world around me. If I tried to do that I would only succumb.

I was also learning to pray. Praying is bringing to the Lord everything that troubles and distresses us. It means leaving our burden of cares with Him and going on without it. That day I had been very stupid: I had gathered up all my cares, and after prayer the burden had seemed twice as heavy as it had before. And so I prayed, "Lord, teach me to cast all my burdens upon Thee and go on without them. Only Thy Spirit can teach me that lesson. Give me Thy Spirit, O Lord, and I shall have faith, such faith that I shall no longer carry a load of care."

I read on for a moment in my Bible: "How much more shall your heavenly Father give the Holy Spirit to them that ask him?"

Comforted, I went on.

Barracks 28

One evening, after we had been in the quarantine barracks for several weeks, we were ordered to fall in and move to Barracks 28. "We shall certainly be more comfortable there," we told one another. It was wonderful to be leaving this dreadful Barracks 8.

We stood for hours, and then marched to the new barracks. Before going inside we again had to wait. Our new quarters presented a dismal aspect. Many of the windowpanes were missing, and some of the frames had been stuffed with paper or rags. Looking in, we saw a picture of indescribable filth. Many of the beds showed missing slats. Our brave Mrs. Boileu tried to comfort me, saying, "Keep courage, we shall get through this also."

As we crept closely together in our narrow, dirty beds, some of the women at once fell through their upper beds, bringing down with them a horrible mess of filth and straw. There was little ventilation in the room, and the air was foul. This was to be our home for many months.

One Who Scattered Blessings

It was evening, several weeks later. The barracks were dark. Many of the women were already asleep. A latecomer crawled over me. She had been working long hours in the *Revier* and was dead tired, but she sat down beside me. I had really felt like sleeping too, but had waited for her as I did every evening. It was the most wonderful moment of the day. Out of her pocket she took potatoes, cooked and skinned, and gave one to each of us. That was a potato given with love; how good it tasted!

The other women went to sleep, but we talked a while longer. How much she had done that day! She was a woman who shone with an inner light. She was physically not strong, yet she worked until very late because she saw opportunities for helping many people. She managed to feed many who were hungry, and found clothing for many who were cold. She was a brave woman. When no one bathed certain shockingly filthy patients, she took upon herself this duty of the nurses. She worked like an angel among wicked people, egoists, brutes, deceivers and sadists, and stood by to help everyone who was suffering. And that meant something in Ravensbruck. She always had a friendly word for everyone who happened to need it. One day I saw her go with beaming face to a gypsy girl whom we all avoided because she was so very dirty and because she stole so cleverly.

"My dear child, I am so glad to see you again," and she kissed the little gypsy face. The somber eyes of the girl lighted up and laughed happily. My friend told me that evening that it was not at all strange that the child was dishonest, for she had been sent out at the age of five to steal, and was beaten if she had not stolen enough. "And in the cell," she went on, "the child often asked others, 'Please tell me about the child Jesus; I like to hear about Him.'"

Rebelliousness

I was shoveling sand. The weather was cold but bright. A distant view of hills, lakes, and woods tempted me to stop now and then to lean on my shovel and enjoy the landscape. I drank in the colors. Birds were flying above my head; the skies were blue. In the valley women were chopping down small trees and carrying them away. As they walked, each one with a tree over her shoulder, they reminded me of the walking forest in Shakespeare's *Macbeth*; and I recited: "Till Birnam wood remove to Dunsinane."

I was feeling cheerful and spunky that day. A German supervisor warned me to keep working. She had done that before; and now I did something very risky. I asked her: "What is your number? I am getting tired of your driving me. I shall work as long as I can, but now and then I must rest." I took hold of her sleeve and read her number. I had not the slightest intention of doing anything, but the effect was amazing.

An *Aufseherin* came up, and the woman said to her apprehensively: "That Hollander asked for my number. Why do you suppose she did that?"

The *Aufseherin* did not reply, but beckoned the woman to follow her. A bit farther away she whispered to her. When a little later the supervisor started to come toward me again because I was not working, the *Aufseherin* pulled on her sleeve and together they walked away. This incident, I'm sure, will be unique in the story of Ravensbruck. For we were completely in the power of people who fawned upon those above them and trampled on those beneath them. We were beneath them.

In the Siemens Factory

Betsie and I had been called up for the work crew at the Siemens factory. After early morning roll call we fell into ranks with more than a thousand others and marched out of the gate. We passed the lake, with its waving reeds and the picturesque village on the opposite shore. What a joy it was to see a beautiful landscape after the monochrome gray and black of the camp!

We were put to work in a large factory barracks. It was dull and monotonous work, sorting screws. The room still had to be adapted to factory use. There was no heat, and we crept, shivering, to the window to pick up some of the warmth of the sun's rays. After a couple of hours we were ordered to push wagons to the station. There we had to unload iron plates out of boxcars and bring them to the factory. The iron was so cold that it hurt our hands, and I pressed a wad of wood chips into Betsie's hands to protect them when she took hold of it. The work was much too heavy for both of us.

After the morning's work was over we entered a large barracks for lunch. There we were kept waiting for quite a long time. As I stood leaning against a table I fell asleep. Strange to sleep standing up; I had not known it was possible. Then I dreamed, and suddenly found myself at home in the dining room. I walked through the room, running my hands over the furniture, and then stepped into the kitchen. There I found my sister. I talked to her, telling her that we were doing well, that things were often hard and difficult, but that we were being wonderfully strengthened.

"I had not expected that you would be back so soon," said she. She didn't seem at all surprised, but asked: "Wouldn't you like to walk through the house?"

So I followed her up the stairs. I saw the old paintings, ran my hand over the antique cupboard, and stood at the window for a minute looking out. How natural everything was, and yet how wonderful. I was so completely at home here. It was, of course, where I belonged. I looked into the workroom, chatted with the repairman and the girl in the shop, examined the window display, and checked on the amount of repair work to be done. Back in the dining room I sat for a minute in Father's chair beside the open fireplace.

"Tell me how the children are, and everyone else," I asked. Everything was fine. All were doing well, but were longing ardently for the end of the war and for our return. Then I looked at a photo on the buffet, and with a start I was awake.

I found myself still standing against the table in the lunchroom barracks of Siemens. Betsie was standing beside me. I told her about my dream and then laid my head on her shoulder and sobbed. It had been so wonderful to be at home, but it was all a dream, and this present reality was so very hard. It was one of the rare moments in which homesickness had got the better of me.

I stepped back into the long line of factory workers returning to the work barracks.

Amazing Guidance

Our supervisor was a sweet young Czech. She helped us along in a kind way and tried to shift the heaviest work away from us. She had great confidence in my skill after she heard that my vocation was that of a watchmaker, and promised to look for some intricate and interesting work for me. Working at Siemens was harder than we had expected. Immediately after the long, early-morning roll call came the march to the factory, and then eleven hours of work. And here things were not as they were in Vught. There I could sleep now and then if I was tired; and it always rested me wonderfully, even if it was but a short nap. That made it possible for me to keep going. Here everything was under rigid control. Supervision was uninterrupted, and there was not a minute's chance to rest. We were weak and undernourished and, besides that, had another great handicap—we were not given enough time to wash well and to get the lice out of our clothing, which was a time-consuming job. We prayed for relief.

One morning Betsie and I had to go back to the camp with an *Aufseherin*. There we were examined for a certain transport. Naked, we walked past the doctor. Betsie was at once rejected: too weak. I was approved. I stood gazing around in despair. Now we would be parted. Betsie would remain behind alone, and I would be taken to some faraway munitions plant. And Betsie was so dependent on me. She seemed to need my companionship as would a child. If at any time I stayed away too long she would say, "Do not leave me alone so long." It was as though I was her hiding place in this evil environment.

A woman doctor examined my eyes; I told her that I could not see well, and pretended not to be able to distinguish the words when I was asked to read.

"Do you want to be rejected?" she asked.

"Yes," I answered, "I want to stay with my sister, who is very weak and needs my support."

"I'll see what I can do for you."

She made an appointment for my return the next day to get another pair of glasses, and set the time for the very hour that the transport was to leave for the munitions plant. So the danger was averted for the time being, but my name would certainly appear on the list for the next transport.

The following day I went to the *Revier* to be examined for the new glasses, but a *Lagerpolizei*[31] would not let me in. "You are not allowed to go to the hospital at this hour without an escort. Your *Stube-älteste* will have to bring you." Back I went and asked The Snake to go with me. We called her that partly because she wore a dress that reminded us of snakeskin, but also because of her deceitful character.

"I haven't the time," said she, "ask the other *Stube-älteste*."

To the other side of the block I went; but the other *Stube-älteste* had no time either. In a quandary I returned to Betsie. "What shall I do? Just wait? Let's pray for guidance." Only a few minutes later someone shouted, "Report for the knitting commando!"

We stepped forward, were enrolled, and were both given wool and knitting needles. "How wonderful!" We were now registered in a commando in which one did not have to work too hard. We merely had to knit; moreover, we also had to remain on our beds because there was nowhere else we could sit. The limited number of stools at the table in the *Stube*, the anteroom of our sleeping-barracks, had been taken quickly by other knitters. They had to work under supervision, while those in the dormitory were comparatively free. It was not long before we laid our knitting aside and used our full time for spiritual work. There were many who needed help and comfort, and I preached twice every day. I now had ample time for it.

I was summoned once more to go for glasses. This time I was successful in getting through to the doctor. She held office hours in a narrow corridor, where she had placed her eye-test chart on a small stool. After trying on several different pairs of glasses, I said to her:

"My own glasses are adequate for knitting, but I could not see well enough with them to do close factory work. However, I have meanwhile been put into the knitting commando."

"Well, then," said she, "you may go back. We haven't many glasses, and you will very likely remain in the knitting commando." Her stock consisted entirely of stolen glasses, so there was only an incomplete assortment.

I was happy to be outside the range of any subsequent transport, although there could be no certainty about it. I should always be in danger as long as I was in the power of this evil regime.

The Red Card

One evening as we were lying asleep, Betsie and I were called. Now what? Hurriedly we slipped on some clothing and went up in front. The clerk said: "You're both to go back to Siemens tomorrow."

With an air of great surprise I answered: "But that's impossible; we are both in the knitting commando."

Without another word she scratched us off the list and we heard nothing more about it. Before dismissing us, however, she gave us each a red card. These cards classified us as being unfit for heavy work. Gratefully we crept back into bed. Perhaps Ravensbruck would not be too bad after all. The next morning I heard that whenever the camp became overcrowded, those holding red cards were gassed.

Sick Transport

It was dark on the *Lagerstrasse*. Arc lamps glowed dimly in the blackness. A cold, heavy mist kept the light rays from penetrating any great distance. Each morning roll call was a recurrent torment. Regardless of the weather, we were kept standing at attention for hours, in ranks of ten. The rain drenched us so that our clothes remained wet for days. Those who stood on the edges suffered especially from the cold wind. If we happened to be standing in a puddle of water we were not allowed to move out of it, although our footwear was in wretched condition and wet feet were a major contributing factor in the great prevalence of intestinal diseases.

It looked as though it were freezing today, and we stamped our feet from the cold. Thousands of stamping feet were beating rhythmically in the darkness and silence of early morning. Except for an occasional snarl from the *Aufseherinnen*, it was the only sound we heard.

Suddenly we heard another and unfamiliar sound. Trucks were coming up the street, stopping just opposite us. They were flat freight trucks without canvas tops. Now the door of the hospital barracks opened and we saw a nurse come out with someone leaning on her arm. She helped the woman up on the truck and laid her down. Others followed. The nurse remained standing on the truck and helped those who seemed to be too weak to take the big step without assistance. From mouth to mouth went the terrifying word: "Sick transport!"

The stamping of feet had ceased. Horror-stricken, we watched the scene before our eyes. We all knew that there was no return from that trip. Were all of those women going to be gassed? It was simply inconceivable. The nurse skilfully helped the sick to lie or sit as comfortably as possible. A hundred patients were divided between the two trucks. Among them were the feebleminded, the incurables and even a few merely troublesome patients. One of them was a mother whose small son was also in the camp. She pleaded so persistently with everyone who approached her to bring her son to her that she had come to be a great nuisance; and now here she was, lying on one of the transport trucks. The trucks moved away, headed toward the brick building at the foot of the great square smokestack, and disappeared into the mist. The door of the hospital barracks closed.

Sociability

Three of us were sitting on our narrow cot. "Polletje," a most charming little woman, was slicing our bread. She could work miracles with our scanty rations. She sliced the bread thinly, covered it with slices of cold, boiled potato, and then sprinkled it with minced onion and salt. We had traded three days' ration of bread for the onion and salt. That reduced our portion of bread considerably, but it tasted so much better. She passed these "tarts" to each one of us on a newspaper, and she had a way of serving things so appetizingly and with such social grace that it tasted wonderfully good.

"I think I'll go on eating potato and onion on my bread even after I'm at home," said I.

My remark turned Polletje's thoughts toward home, and she began to tell us about her dogs. How she loved them! And she knew much about them, for she was a well-known authority on dogs. Even her face revealed the fact that she was the dog-loving type. She told about her small villa surrounded by a flower garden, and I read homesickness in her eyes. Poor Polletje, she was never to see it again.

Betsie and I were sitting on our bed talking. It was dark. The window nearest us now had all its panes out but two. The occupants of the upper beds would kick against the window in climbing down and break the panes. It was entirely unavoidable. Now there was a blanket in front of the window, and it was darker than ever; but there was such a cold wind that we could not leave the window uncovered. I wondered if the last two panes would break also? If they did it would be pitch dark in here, and that would be very bad. Our spirits were so dependent on light. If the day were sunny, I felt hopeful; if it rained, everything was dismal, and we fell an easy prey to worries and fears.

My arm was thrown around Betsie and I could feel that her heartbeat was weak and rapid. I had observed that before.

The Miracle of the Vitamins

Upon entering the camp we had to surrender not only our clothing but also our medicines. But we were allowed to keep a few toilet articles. My small bottle of Davitamon, a liquid vitamin compound, was then about half full. I set it down on the table, and the woman who was checking us in said: "That is also a toilet article."

She put it back into my bag with her own hands, and I was very happy about it. Vitamin deficiency was one of the gravest hazards to the prisoners. From the very first day I gave everyone sleeping around me a couple of drops of Davitamon daily. I gave it to as many as thirty persons at a time, but the little bottle continued to yield its drops. This went on for six or eight weeks, until the women no longer asked me, "Do you still have some Davitamon?" but, "Do you still have any oil from the cruse of the widow of Zarephath?"

They were right in calling it that, for, as "the jar of meal wasted not, neither did the cruse of oil fail, according to the word of Jehovah which He spake by Elijah" (1Kings 17:16, ASV) so also were we experiencing a like miracle.

Then one day my friend who worked in the hospital brought me a bag full of vitamins; I believe it was brewers' yeast. "Give this to all the women around you," said she. "There is so much vitamin deficiency in camp. But do not tell anyone that I gave it to you." So I gave each woman enough to last her for a week.

That evening I said to Betsie, "I am going to give you Da-vitamon too as long as it lasts." But not a drop came out of the bottle. The miracle was no longer necessary.

The bag of vitamins was also blessed. There always seemed to be enough, until one evening someone asked me, "Do you still have some vitamins?" "No," said I, "I am very sorry, but it is all gone."

I still had a tiny bit left, but wanted to keep it for Betsie. Now I confessed to her, "That really showed that I was lacking in faith. I should have been more confident and have given her the last little bit." Scarcely were the words out of my mouth when I saw my friend from the hospital approaching. And she actually had another bagful of vitamins with her. It was a great miracle. Vitamins were hard to get throughout the entire camp. Even if a doctor felt they were necessary for some patient he wanted to favor he would still frequently be unable to procure them. It is really not out of place to speak of "the miracle of the vitamins."

Plans

It was evening in Barracks 28. Many were already asleep. A feeble ray of light reached our bed. The one electric light bulb was against the ceiling towards the front of the room and illumined only a few beds.

Betsie and I were discussing plans for the future. After our return to Holland we would renovate our house. We had already invited many people to come to our home, for there were very many women here who were going to find themselves without home or furniture, family or money. They would, of course, be taken care of by various organizations and societies, but there would be some, especially among the young people, in need of a home where they would also receive some measure of guidance.

We had no garden, which was a pity, but perhaps we could build a roof garden later on; or perhaps purchase the house at the back of us and plan a garden there. If our house was too small we would have to move out of town. We had to have a roomy, pleasant house, for it was a real home we wished to establish.

Then there must be a beautiful, large, modern clubhouse in the middle of Haarlem. We would have to give a good deal of thought and attention to the disrupted youth of our country. All of those boys and girls who had been doing such responsible and dangerous work must be given an opportunity to grow young again. There would be an athletic field, a gymnasium and a beautiful room for plays and folk dances and for showing really good films, and cozily furnished rooms and offices for the club workers.

There must be a central-heating system, but also open fireplaces for wood fires. Betsie and I would tour America, picking up some new ideas, lecturing here and there and telling of the marvelous way the Lord has blessed and kept us, and of the miracles we have experienced. If there are persons who cannot endure the anxieties and cares of life we shall tell them that Jesus is the victor. We shall be well qualified to speak on that subject. No one will be able to say, "It's easy for you to talk." "Persecution, oppression, hunger, nakedness . . . in all these things we are more than conquerors through Him who loved us."

After the light was out we still lay a long time, huddled under our coats and blanket, whispering about our plans. Then we fell asleep and dreamed of the day of freedom which was sure to come.

Murder in the Barracks

I was listening to what was going on behind me. Old Mrs. Leness had not been able to get up for roll call that morning and had stayed in bed. The *Lagerpolizei* came at once and dragged her out. These camp police were fellow prisoners who had been appointed to keep order outside on the street and at times also in the barracks. There were good people among them, but most of them were cruel.

After they had pulled Mrs. Leness out of bed it was obvious that she could not stand. So they beat her, and left her lying exhausted on the floor. We found her there after roll call, stiff from the cold and deathly sick. We carried her to her bed, and now she was growing steadily worse and very weak. We had asked for a stretcher to carry her to the hospital, but nothing was done about it. I heard her moaning quietly.

The week before I had talked with her about the love of the Savior. "You must give Him your heart, for He bore your sins also on the cross." "Yes," she had said then, "but I have so little faith."

"Then pray as did the father of the demon-possessed boy. 'Lord, I believe; help Thou mine unbelief.' We do not need a great faith, but faith in a great Savior."

Then she had smiled, and we thanked the Lord that His strength was fulfilled in weakness. She was a frail, nervous woman, who was badly in need of nursing and friendly, loving care. The other Hollanders were fortunately good to her, and I saw that they were carrying her to the toilet room. But on the way something dreadful happened. An *Aufseherin* saw that she had soiled herself and beat her hard and cruelly, leaving her lying on the floor.

The Snake, our *Stube-älteste*, climbed abruptly to one of the upper beds and ordered a young, pregnant woman to follow her outside. She took her to another barracks, saying, "You don't have to look at that." Was there still something like concern for others in The Snake?

It was deathly quiet in our room. It was too awful. Someone cried out suddenly, "She's dying!" and then, "Now it's all over." I felt sick from the horror of it, and looked at Betsie to see if it had affected her in the same way. But her face was serene and her eyes had a faraway look in them. She had been mercifully oblivious to the entire incident. I had observed before that dreadful things about which she could do nothing did not penetrate to her soul.

"Hast Thou not made an hedge about Job?" came to my mind. Around Betsie, too, there was a hedge.

Nocturnal Roll Call

It was night, and we were outside for roll call. The air was heavy with fog. From the barracks to the left of us women were appearing through the mist. For a moment their figures were silhouetted against the glow of light from the door. Suddenly I shivered from the cold and the misery. Those women were coming out of the *Nacht-und-Nebelbarak* (or "detention barracks"). They were not allowed to hear a word from home or to receive parcels; no one was even supposed to know that they were there.

That was really no worse than our own experience, but they had been living under such conditions for so long. Some of them were under sentence of death. In the same barracks lived also the *Kanienchen* (or "guinea pigs"). These were the women who were condemned to death and were to be used for vivisection. I was once in their barracks. It was much cleaner than ours, and there were tables and stools. Many of the women were sitting there sewing or writing, and there was an agreeable atmosphere in the room. I could never understand how people in such circumstances could adjust themselves so well and remain so normal.

I didn't understand prisoners at all. Did I understand myself? Was I that same human being who had lived in comparative luxury, protected and pampered and revelling in all that art, culture and loving friends so abundantly provided? The cold fog penetrated through my clothing. I felt in my pocket for some scraps of paper torn from a newspaper and put them under my dress over my shoulders to keep out, if possible, some of the cold. Paper does help to keep out the cold, but these pieces were too small.

I was now experiencing one of those moments in which I was painfully aware of my poverty and my imprisonment. Fortunately, I was not always so keenly conscious of it. Around me I saw thousands of prisoners. How many of them, I wondered, were feeling their misery at this moment as I was?

The Guardhouse

As we fell in line for the knitting commando in the morning, we passed the guardhouse. All the camp barracks were gray and dreary-looking, but this one was worse than all the others. At times we would see its unfortunate inmates standing in the courtyard between the two barracks, behind the bars that separated it from the street. Many of the women and girls would stand at the bars, clutching them with both hands. They looked like caged animals. They would call out to us as we passed. Looking closely, we could see that there were refined girls and women among them, but most of them belonged to the underworld of the various countries they represented. The *Lagerpolizei* kept a regular guard on duty along the street outside the courtyard. If the women called out to us, she would yell at them; and if we replied she would beat us, raving and cursing. At times we came by when the women were away at work. The hardest and heaviest work in camp was reserved for them—chopping wood, carrying coal and building roads.

Whenever the courtyard was deserted there was always one young girl left, and she was the personification of the misery of Ravensbruck! Huddled against the wall, she was a picture of abject misery. When it rained she crept under an old door which leaned against the wall and gave her some small degree of shelter. I never saw her face, because she sat hunched up, like a sick animal; but her body was so wasted it looked like a skeleton.

Why she sat there I did not know; nor did I ask. One does not ask such questions in a concentration camp. But I breathed a silent prayer for her as I passed by.

"O Savior, full of mercy, take this poor child into Your arms; comfort her, and make her happy."

No one was ever cheerful in Ravensbruck. And that was not because of his own suffering; one learned to accept that, and a human being has amazing powers of adjustment. But to see a child such as this one sitting in the courtyard robbed one of all ability and desire to laugh! When I was very small and heard for the first time the story of the scapegoat, laden with the guilt of Israel and brought far out into the desert, so far that he could never find his way back to the camp, I felt great sympathy for him. And, though I did not attempt to reason why, each time I passed this child I was reminded of the scapegoat. I felt such deep sorrow whenever I saw her. She was no doubt a feebleminded child, and I comforted myself with the thought that, after I was free, I would establish a home for backward folk, a bright, sunny home, filled with flowers and color and love.

A girl was once being beaten in the guardhouse. I was lying on the path behind it that first night of our stay in the camp. The screams of the girl were regular, as regular as the blows that fell on her body. They were not the kind of blows we were familiar with—struck in uncontrolled fury by one brutal woman or another. This was the execution of a formal sentence, a fixed number of lashes. A doctor stood by to direct the wielder of the lash where to strike, in order not to damage any vital part of the body. The stretcher, for carrying her to the hospital afterwards, stood ready.

Children in Ravensbruck

A beam of sunlight was shining in upon the blond curls of a five-year-old girl. I could scarcely take my eyes from her; she was very pretty and had such a happy little face. Hand in hand, she stood with her dark-eyed little friend of four, singing Jewish child melodies.

Their voices were pure and sweet, but they sounded out of place here. These little children belonged in a playroom or a sunny flower garden. They looked neat and clean; even here their mothers managed to do some sewing for them in their free time, and took good care of them.

At that time children did not have to appear for roll call at night, but no one knew how long it would last. The order might come at any time that they, too, would have to appear with the grown-ups. They would then have to stand out in the night under the starry heavens. Their little feet would stamp from the cold. And they would not be able to understand why they should wait so long before going inside.

Now, however, they stayed behind, quietly sleeping in their beds in the large barracks. During roll call they were alone with an eight-year-old brother. One morning the boy had a temper tantrum. He stamped his small feet on the ground and said: "Mammie can't do that, Mammie may not do that; it is much too heavy work for her."

His mother had been called for the sand-digging commando, which was, indeed, much too heavy work for her. The little fellow stood in helpless fury, and then went sobbing to the table where lessons were beginning. On the narrow edges of a newspaper, a woman was teaching the children to do their sums.

Discord

A quarrel was going on in the room. A Polish woman and a Belgian were lying together on a cot $27^{1}/_{2}$ inches wide. Is it a wonder that conflicts arose? Even with people of our own type we still had to be careful to respect their feelings and to take them sufficiently into consideration. The women were screaming at each other, fighting and trying to throw each other off the bed. Others meddled in the quarrel, and the shouting grew louder.

Betsie seized my arm. "We must pray, Corrie; only the Lord can help us." And then she prayed, "Lord, remove this spirit of contention from the room. It is too strong for these poor people. They are so unhappy and so irritated. But Thou art the conqueror. Let Thy grace touch the hearts of these women. Let Thy Spirit fill our souls."

Like a storm that is stilled, the voices subsided; a cry or two, and all was quiet. How great is the power of prayer! When we expect much from the Lord, He gives us much.

Heavy Work

It was Sunday morning in late October. It had been cold during roll call, and we were waiting to get back into the barracks. We never felt quite so impoverished as during those minutes we were waiting to go inside. So little had been left to us, and when we were even temporarily deprived of the roof over our heads our sense of deprivation reached a climax. Our beds were dirty and full of lice; the floor was indescribably filthy; there was but little light inside, because more windowpanes were broken and replaced by cardboard or, if all the panes of a window were out, by a blanket. It was not an attractive shelter; but as we stood outside we longed to have those walls about us and that roof over our heads. Even an animal needs a nest or den. If only we could go inside we could rest, and get warm. Standing was so wearisome in our undernourished condition.

Someone pulled at my arm. "*Arbeitseinsatz*,"[32] snarled a woman. She had a whip in her hand and pushed me in the direction of a group of prisoners standing in ranks of five. I looked around to see if I could still escape, but it was impossible. Our numbers had been taken; it would be obvious that I had run away and I would be sure to get a summons, which was the terror of us all.

On the great open square we waited. Mien was standing beside me. She had been discharged from the hospital the day before, though she still had a high fever. The doctor had cleared out the hospital and discharged everyone whose temperature was below 39 degrees centigrade (102.2 degrees Fahrenheit). I only hoped we would not be given heavy work.

"*Alle Beutel abgeben!*" (Turn in your bags!) And they took away the bags containing our meager possessions. We always carried about with us everything we owned because there was so much stealing. One old lady refused to give up her bag and held it tightly to her. In her eyes was the terror of a hunted animal. Oh dear, an *Aufseherin* struck her! She defended herself, and was promptly dragged to the officer in charge of the *Arbeitseinsatz*. There must have been something human left in the man, for he scolded the *Aufseherin* saying, "Don't beat these Hollanders. You won't get anywhere with that."

But she screamed indignantly, "That woman struck me." They began to wrangle loudly, but it all ended in the old lady's being reported. From then on she was in constant danger of being summoned for a hearing and of being punished in the bunkers or by the lash. She was a brave woman, but an anxious, haunted look came over her. I suffered with her, for she reminded me of my mother.

Then came the ordeal of passing through the gate. On either side were officers and a number of *Aufseherinnen*. The men looked like wild animals feeding on their prey. When one woman failed to keep her arms stretched out before her, one of the officers pounced on her, dragged her out of the line, and beat her cruelly. It seemed to be nothing more than a fiendish demonstration of his cowardly daring before the others, who looked with pleasure and approval upon his treatment of a weak woman. Another "stalwart" officer pulled a small bag out of the hands of an old woman and threw it on the ground with a curse. What an experience it was to pass through the gate with an "honor guard" of such depraved people on either side of us!

"I shall preserve thy going out and thy coming in," said the Lord to me. I looked up; small, fleecy-white clouds, tinged with red, moved like a flock of sheep across the sky. Then we were on the road. At our left was the lovely lake, with its rustling reeds and a rowboat, and the woods on the opposite shore. Children in neat dresses were out for their Sunday walks. So close to us was there a happy, free, and normal kind of life! It did me good just to look at it—it brought me a measure of inward healing. But an *Aufseherin* gave me a cuff and a command to look straight ahead. I walked with difficulty, for I was no longer accustomed to marching, and my feet and legs were swollen with hunger oedema.[33]

We turned sharply to the right and through a wood. How beautiful it was! I breathed deeply; the winter air smelled good. We halted at a hilly spot where several cars full of potatoes were standing on the rails. With the other women I had to shove the cars ahead. The rough iron wheels were like ice to my hands as we struggled to turn them. When the car started to move, I stumbled and took a step to the side. I was panting from the hard work. An *Aufseherin* saw it and said, sneeringly, "Oh, perhaps the hands of Madam Baroness are too delicate for such work?"

"Madam Baroness"? I looked at myself. My coat was soiled and frayed; the hem was out. I had left it that way because it was much too short. On my hands were parts of a worn-out stocking. My legs were covered with pieces of knitted stuff, tied on with rope; my shoes were completely worn out, the soles dangling loosely, my toes protruding. On my head was a dark-checked, cloth cap. "Madam Baroness"? I was poorer than the poorest beggar in the Netherlands.

A woman shoved a large basket into my hands. She then shoveled potatoes into it, and a Polish prisoner and I had to carry it up the hill. I could scarcely lift it; after twenty steps I stopped and could go no farther.

"*Schneller, aber schneller!*" screamed a forewoman. Forewomen were fellow prisoners who had charge of the division of labor and the tempo at which the work was done, and so bore the responsibility for it. Their wages consisted of an extra allowance of food. If not enough work was done, they were beaten; and fear made them drive us on. German forewomen were usually hard and cruel, walking around with whips in their hands.

I toiled up the hill. There the potatoes were dumped into long trenches. Slowly I walked back; but the Polish woman, with whom I was carrying the basket, pulled me along, looking at me with hostile eyes. She herself was strong and evidently used to hard work; she didn't understand that I was not unwilling, but unable, to move faster. I saw Mien, her face flushed with fever, carrying a heavy basket alone. How energetic she was, in spite of her illness!

Long furrows had been made against a slope, and I walked up carrying a small basket of potatoes. An *Aufseherin* called out something, and five or six women got together and pointed at me in derision. "Look at that; there is a Hollander for you, daring to come up with a little basket of potatoes! She is too lazy to exert herself."

"Say, are you afraid we'll finish too soon?"

"May I empty your basket for you, Madam Baroness?"

The basket was torn out of my hands, emptied and thrown at me. One woman pushed me, and as I walked back I could hear their shrieking laughter following me. I felt only disdain for the women who treated me so. It was no fault of mine that I was weak and unable to walk, but rather the result of the maltreatment of their own countrymen. I thought of One who had endured scorn and derision for me. No, these women could do me no enduring harm, though their sneers were painful to bear. Then I lost my shoe. The sole was nearly off, and my feet were soaking wet. I approached an *Aufseherin* who was flirting with an officer. He had just given her a cigarette. I stood at attention.

"Number sixty-six thousand, seven hundred and thirty, Prisoner ten Boom, Cornelia, reporting."

Every time I uttered this prescribed introduction to a request I had an almost irresistible impulse to laugh.

"What do you want?" she asked, between puffs on her cigarette.

"May I stop working?" I asked politely. "I can't keep it up; my shoes are completely worn out."

She was such a young thing, about the age of my club girls at home. I wondered if it would be possible to organize clubs with such girls later on. They would be too demoralized, I thought; this life would ruin many.

She looked down at me from her lofty position and snapped, "Go barefooted"; and then in a milder tone, "Take fewer potatoes in your basket if you can't carry more."

What a long day! At lunchtime we had to step forward, five abreast, and were given hot porridge in our mugs. How delicious it was! It warmed me all over, but my legs were trembling from fatigue. Marching back to the camp, I stumbled rather than walked. And then we still had to pass through the gate.

"Lord, help Thou me; preserve my going out and my coming in; I plead upon Thy promises," I prayed. We got safely through. In the barracks I fell exhausted upon my bed. After a half hour of deep sleep I had recovered sufficiently to lead the church service. I spoke on the text: "Be strong in the Lord, and in the power of His might" (Eph. 6:10). What a joy it was to comfort others and myself with the thought that Jesus was the victor, and that His strength was fulfilled in weakness. As I spoke about the great love and mercy of the Savior, I felt myself lifted up and far beyond the camp.

"They that wait upon the LORD shall renew their strength."

General Roll Call

Again it was Sunday. All the prisoners were assembled together. The Hollanders seemed to be in good spirits. One by one we walked past an officer who made notations about us in a book. We stood in line precisely according to number. It was amusing to see how imperturbably, even nonchalantly, the Hollanders passed "his Highness." Each one recited her number and name, showed her sleeve, on which the number was stitched, and moved on into the next group.

The German *Aufseherinnen* in their gray suits were being coquettish. To them the officer was a man. They snapped and sneered in the customary manner at those who made mistakes, but their voices were different. Among the Hollanders and Belgians there was not a semblance of fear or even of being impressed. A

Belgian was knitting; a Hollander was calmly preparing a sandwich; a third was putting her hair up in pincurls with pins she had made in the factory. Another was reading; still another was writing, using the back of the woman in front of her as a desk.

From where I stood I could see the women from the next barracks. There were Polish women and, among them, one was nursing her baby. Children were not allowed to be left in the barracks during general roll call. Poor woman. There she stood, with her little bundle of humanity in her arms. Why, oh why, was she not being tenderly cared for by the baby's father? Was he, perhaps, also a prisoner in a concentration camp? Would her undernourished body be able to provide enough food for her child, or would they both gradually waste away? The tragedy of the place again cut me to the quick. The Hollanders had managed to create a homelike atmosphere about them, wherever they were—a pleasant something which, however small, still seemed to fortify them against their cruel environment. But there was nothing pleasant about Ravensbruck. Ravensbruck was an annihilation camp, a hell!

Covetousness

It was Mieke's birthday. Was it possible that she was already eighteen! She was such a brave little thing. Seriously ill with tuberculosis, she was allowed to spend much of the time in her upper bunk in the *Stube*. We were all very fond of her. Though often homesick, she was always patient and resigned to her situation. Meeting such a person always brought to my lips the agonized prayer to God: "O Lord, how much longer? Save us in Thy mercy!"

Mieke needed hygienic nursing and loving, tender care. And here she had nothing—except love. We all loved her. Colored paper and a couple of real flowers formed the decorations. The birthday cake, a sort of tart made of bread and potatoes, garnished with bits of beet and radishes, looked almost real. And there was even an appetizing salad, toasted bread with onion, beet and potato. The table stood behind a cupboard, and the guests sat crowded together on their little stools. Coming by, I saw the decorated table and stopped to congratulate Mieke, and then remained standing. I was so very hungry, and she waited a few seconds before offering me something. During those seconds I caught myself silently praying a very childish and unworthy prayer: "O Lord, please have them give me a little of that toasted bread." Immediately afterwards they passed me the plate, and I bit into the "tasty tart." How very delicious it was! But there was shame in my heart. Was I becoming egoistic and covetous? Was hunger going to get me down? A few minutes later, before eating our turnip soup, I prayed: "Lord, bless this food for Jesus' sake, Amen."

How often I had prayed those words thoughtlessly! Now they were fraught with meaning. If God's blessing rested on this food it would be enough, and it would also keep me from becoming covetous.

The Ravensbruck That Destroys

When we arrived as newcomers in Ravensbruck we were received by previously interned Hollanders not only with a warm welcome but also with much advice. Among other things they said: "You can hold out here provided you learn to take care only of yourself." At that time I had answered, "That is the Ravensbruck that destroys," which was a variant of the expression made by Selma Lagerlöf: "There is a Jerusalem that destroys."

Now that I had been here for some time I could see what a great danger this camp life was for us spiritually. Egoism would creep into our hearts before we were aware of it, and it was a tenacious devil, most difficult to dislodge. For instance, a sweater was for sale. Who should have it? At once one thought, "I should, because I was so cold this morning." A person was tempted to forget that others needed it just as badly. Need teaches us to pray, but need can also make us selfish. Demons had the upper hand in Ravensbruck. Cruelty and sadism revealed themselves in all their ugliness and gruesomeness. Egoism, by contrast, looked fairly respectable; but I fear that, for us, it was an even greater danger.

Shoveling Sand

I once explained to a class of feebleminded girls the difference between *creating* and *making*, and encountered an amusing but apt pun. I had explained very carefully that when one built a house, he needed stone, wood and many other things, but that God had created the world out of nothing. A week later I asked: "Does anyone remember what creating (*scheppen*) is?"

Now *scheppen* is not only the Dutch word for creating, it also means shoveling. And one of the girls, confusing these two entirely unrelated meanings of the word, said: "That is simple, *'Als wij scheppen, hebben wij een scheppie nodig; God kan scheppen zonder scheppie'*" (When we shovel we need a shovel; God can shovel without a shovel).

Now Betsie and I were shoveling sand. A certain area had to be graded. The dirt was shoveled from one pile to another until it reached the hollows it was intended to fill. It was very cold. In spite of the heavy work, we felt the icy wind penetrate our clothing. There was a beautiful view of hills, woods and ponds. We were outside the camp, but there was no question of escape. Where could we go? We were deep in the heart of wicked Germany. Moreover, there were guards all around us. The "Gray Mice," *Aufseherinnen*, all carried straps which they used as whips. Even the forewomen were armed with them and used them to drive us on. If we stopped for a second to catch our breath, they would rush at us. Betsie took only small amounts of sand on her shovel because she was not strong enough to do more. It was such a pity that she had to do this heavy work. An *Aufseherin* ordered her to take larger shovelfuls, but she answered quietly, "Just let me go on this way; then perhaps I can keep it up. If I take more hay on my fork I shall merely have to quit sooner." And then there were three of the slave drivers standing beside her, taunting her and pointing in derision at her slow pace. They could be so viciously insulting.

If only they did not beat her! All her life she had been carefully surrounded with loving attention. And now, when she was weaker than ever before, she had to do this hard work among these evil people. No, they could not, they must not, beat her!

She was working with her back toward me. Suddenly she turned around and said, with a twinkle in her eye: "*God kan scheppen zonder scheppie*" (God can shovel without a shovel). Betsie never lost her sense of humor. I saw then that she was undisturbed by the evil about her. Her face was peaceful and serene, as always. And my heart spoke, "Lord, '*Gij kunt scheppen zonder scheppie.*' Thou art all-powerful. I do not know what to do; Thou knowest all things. Everything necessary to our welfare has been taken from us. But Thou art the Creator; Thou canst create well-being, though all physical conditions for it are lacking."

The unintentional pun of a feebleminded girl had become the refrain of my pleading before God.

"*Schneller, aber schneller!*" snarled an *Aufseherin*. She cracked her whip across my back; but in my heart there was peace.

"The Light" Won

We were all undernourished, for the food was hopelessly inadequate. Our warm meal consisted of turnips or pumpkins, cooked in a large quantity of water. The caraway seeds which were cooked in it did not make it more tasty. One of the effects of our constant feeling of hunger was the tendency to talk incessantly about food. The finest recipes were dictated to interested listeners.

"I know a wonderful way of baking cheesecakes." "Do you want a recipe for a tasty pudding? You take a half pint of cream, a cup of sugar, the juice of four oranges. . . ." So they planned what they would eat after they were free, but the turnip soup no longer tasted good.

Betsie and I decided never to talk about food. We had observed that there were many demons in our environment and were reminded of the text: "This kind can come forth by nothing, but by prayer and fasting." We decided to link up our involuntary fasting with our spiritual endeavors. The result was that we did not suffer because of the poor food; it even tasted good much of the time. The blessings we received upon our struggle against the evil powers around us we ascribed to our fasting. It was so wonderful that we had contact with a loving Savior. We talked it over with Him and, though we did not clearly understand this problem ourselves, we left it in His hands and worked quietly on. We often experienced the opposition of the devil.

One day news reached us that a young woman in Hospital Barracks 8 had lost courage completely. That was really alarming, for we had often observed that when the will to live was gone the body soon gave up the battle also. We decided to make an effort to get through to her somehow. Visiting in the hospital was strictly forbidden, but five of us went over there. In a corner near the barracks we held a simple prayer meeting. Then I set out. I knew which window was nearest her bed, but saw at once that the shutters were closed.

I went back and we prayed together: "Lord, wilt Thou cause the shutters to be opened." A *Lagerpolizei* passed the barracks and opened the shutters. Again I went over and stood next to her window, but now there was a new difficulty—the window could not be opened from the outside. So once more I went back to my friends and we prayed together that the window might be opened. Before I got back a Polish woman had opened the window from the inside.

Then I began my conversation: "Willy, can you hear me?"

"Oh, yes, how wonderful that you have come! I am so discouraged. I have such dreadful pain, and everything is equally depressing."

Whack! A *Lagerpolizei* slapped me. "Move on!" she snarled.

Back to my friends I went. "Lord wilt Thou keep the *Lagerpolizei* away from me and give me comforting words for Willy," I prayed. Then I went back and stood a bit farther from the window. The *Lagerpolizei* was nowhere to be seen.

"Willy, remember that the Lord Jesus loves you. When you have pain, think about His sufferings, which He bore for your sins and to direct you on the road to heaven. That is why the suffering of this present time is not to be measured against the glory which is to come. If you take hold of the Savior's hand He will keep you close to Him and help you through, and then this tribulation will work for you an eternal weight of glory." I continued speaking quietly to her in this manner for a little while, until she finally called out: "Now I see things clearly again. It is all gloriously true, and my courage has come back. You have comforted me. Thank you very much."

Whack! Another slap from the *Lagerpolizei*! She banged down the window and closed the shutters. Further conversation was impossible, but I knew that Jesus had again conquered and that Willy was comforted. Back in our corner near the barbed wire fence we thanked God that evil had not won.

More Than Conquerors in Christ

After roll call Betsie and I usually slept a little longer. We were always so thoroughly chilled and tired out that we had to creep under our blankets and coats to recuperate. One day we were not allowed to go back into the barracks but had to go to the delousing tent. It was an enormous tent, large enough to hold thousands of people. The floor was of stone, and there was not a place to sit. It was a cold day; the wind was howling and the rain coming down in torrents. We had to undress and allow our bodies and all our clothing to be sprinkled with insect powder. It made us wretchedly dirty and stuck to our hands. We felt cold and tired, sick and miserable.

"I cannot conduct a meeting today," I said to Betsie. I stood with my arm about her. "No," said she, "I can understand that."

Then we saw in a corner of the tent a group of Polish women holding a religious service. They were listening devoutly. And the Lord told me that I, too, should speak that day. Calling a couple of acquaintances, I said to them: "After the Poles have finished their mass we'll meet in the same place. Will you pass the word around?"

That day our group consisted not only of those who came every day but also of many others, who came, perhaps out of sheer boredom. Then I began to speak. I knew that I was weak, unequal to the difficulties—the cold, the misery and the fatigue. But God spoke through His Spirit. Those who had never come before I urged to repent, and I testified to the victory of Jesus Christ.

How amazing! I had never before been so keenly aware of my weakness; but still I could speak with fervency and conviction. "More than conqueror in Christ." It was very clear to me that only the work of the Holy Spirit had triumphed here, His strength through my weakness.

"You looked like a Salvation Army lass," said one of my friends to me later.

Several of my listeners who had never worshiped with us before now became faithful attendants.

After our service was finished, the Catholic Hollanders and Belgians gathered for the reading of their mass. It was November 1, and they were celebrating All Saints' Day. Their gathering was large, and their prayers were fervent. And that day, a day so full of misery, became a demonstration to the honor and glory of God.

The Word Takes Its Course

We were not the only ones being used by the Lord to spread the gospel. The others, however, could not preach. Should I say rather that they did not feel called upon to do so, although I am sure some of them could have done so very well.

One of us had a psalter hymnal. She loaned it regularly to others and many were helped by it. How beautiful the Psalms are, and the old *gezangen*[34] too! Never before had I appreciated them as much as now. The owner of the hymnal also talked frequently to others about the Savior; and sometimes, after I had spoken, she would take part in a dialogue with me in which she cooperated wonderfully. Everyone then listened, and she often gave a very pertinent supplement to my remarks. Her conversations with me alone were always edifying, and it was a joy to stand beside her at roll call.

I knew also that several of the young people who had been taken away on the various transports had their Bibles hidden in their clothing. Some of them, I was sure, would not keep them for themselves alone, but would use them for others. I wondered if I should ever hear about it later. God's kingdom is coming, and He uses whom He will for that purpose.

> *It is Thy cause, O Lord and King,*
> *The cause for which we stand:*
> *And since it is Thy cause, we know*
> *'Tis safe within Thine hand.*

There were many who accepted the message we brought, but also many who were unapproachable. Distress teaches some to pray; it hardens others. Hardness is a defense mechanism which had at times its temptations for me also. If one cannot endure the sight of the suffering about him he tries to build a cloak of armor about his heart. But that makes him insensitive to good influences also. Would these people, once grown insensitive, change when they were again in better circumstances? I did not know. God has a special path for each individual.

I did not experience any marked hostility among my fellow prisoners. Even those who did not agree with me remained friendly. I was very thankful for that.

Hell

It was dreadfully cold at roll call this morning. Though it was not supposed to start until 4:30, we were driven from our beds at 3:30. One morning three women from Barracks 28 had lingered inside a few minutes to avoid the cold. All the following week the entire barracks was punished by an extra hour at attention. The camp lights were not even lit when we came out into the *Lagerstrasse*. This was the street where all the prisoners assembled and stood at attention. It was said that there were then approximately thirty-five thousand people present. It seemed today that there would be no end to it; and when finally the *uhle* (siren) gave the signal to fall out, we were stiff and numb with the cold. It was going to be wonderful to creep back into bed and rest and get warm. But we found the barracks door locked. For forty-five minutes more we were kept standing outside, yearning to be let in.

The *Aufseherin*, meanwhile, guarded the door with a whip. One woman tried to get inside through a window, but was beaten back. The *Block-älteste* beat her unmercifully. I heard the swishing and the groaning, and stood by motionless. I seemed petrified with misery.

A feebleminded girl just in front of us suddenly had an evacuation. The poor child could not help it, and she was wearing only a shirt and dress. But she was brutally beaten. Her screams rose in piercing shrieks. An old woman pleaded to be admitted, but was refused; a few minutes later she collapsed and fell to the ground. I looked at the faces around me, and could read horror and hate on some of them; on others a numb resignation and, on many, despair.

Betsie stood leaning against me; my arms were thrown about her. It was one of the few times when she observed and was vulnerable to the misery around her. Softly she whispered, "Oh, Corrie, this is hell."

"God has promised, 'I will never leave thee nor forsake thee,'"
I whispered back.

The sky suddenly reddened. The sun had not yet risen, but
the clouds, driven before the wind, caught its rays from beneath
the horizon, and reflected a ruddy glow on the earth. Even dark
clouds, illuminated by the sun, spread light and color over everything. "So will the light from our Savior shine on us here in
Ravensbruck, and we shall reflect its color and glow," I said softly.

I did not understand it. Believing is not seeing.

Victory

The uppermost tier of beds was built so close to the ceiling
that one could not sit upright on the beds. Some of the women
had loosened boards from the ceiling, propping them up with
pieces of wood, in order to make head room. It was at one of
these places that I would sit whenever I talked with the younger
women who slept in the upper bunks. Up there the light from the
bulb against the ceiling reached even the farthest beds. All about
me lay many young girls, courageous, sturdy girls. We had been
talking about guidance in our times. Now one of them said: "It
has certainly been no mistake that God directed my life by way
of Ravensbruck. Here, for the first time, I have really learned
to pray. The distress here has taught me that things are never
entirely right in one's life unless he is completely surrendered to
Jesus. I was always rather pious, but there were areas in my life
from which Jesus was completely excluded. Now He is King in
every sphere of my life."

"I had never before realized the seriousness of life until I came
here," said another. "After I am released, my life will be different
from what it was formerly. I have thanked God for sending me
to Ravensbruck."

A girl from the bed behind me pulled on my sleeve and said:
"Please come to us today also; there is a whole group waiting to

hear a Bible message." I crept after her over the beds, bumping my head against the ceiling and catching my dress on the posts of the bunks. There was great happiness in my heart. That Sunday I preached nine times.

"*Arbeitseinsatz antreten!*" (Fall in for work assignment!) Two hundred and fifty young women were selected to go on a transport to Munich. As they formed in ranks in front of the barracks I felt as if something inside me was breaking from grief.

The Name That Is Above Every Name

Whenever large numbers of our Dutch women were sent away on transports they were replaced by Polish women. The latter had suffered a great deal and looked worn and anxious. We could not understand each other's language. Yet we suffered the same affliction side by side. The same Savior had borne their griefs also.

It was evening. A little woman was leaning wearily against the edge of her bed. She looked deeply unhappy. Betsie went to her, took her hand in her own, and said questioningly: "*Jesoes Christoes?*"

A glow of happiness came over the face of the little woman. She drew Betsie to her and kissed her. The Name that is above every name unites not only heaven and earth, but also the hearts of people of different tongues. These Greek Catholic women had such great love for their Savior that the sound of His spoken name made their faces shine.

We sometimes sang, "Come to the Savior, make no delay," and they would sing it with us. The melody of that song had been imported from Poland by the Salvation Army. What the words were in Polish I did not know. Someday we shall sing that song before the throne of God, and there will be no difference of language to separate us.

Separation

Betsie was ill. Her hands felt feverish and her forehead was hot. But she was as cheerful and full of courage as always. Together we went to *zieken-appèl* (roll call for the sick). The inner court of the *Revier* was crowded with hundreds of sick people. Some of them could scarcely stand and leaned heavily on the arms of those less seriously ill. Some were lying on stretchers, out in the cold.

What a cruel thing *zieken-appèl* was! Sometimes the sick had to wait for hours and would thus receive their death blow. It was, however, amazing to see how much a person could endure, even when ill. I thought back to the way our families used to coddle and take care of us at home when there was the slightest thing wrong—how we were allowed to stay in bed, and everything was brought to us that might in any way hasten our recovery. Here we stood outside for hours before being admitted. If one had a high fever of at least 104 degrees or more she was sent to the hospital, only to receive hopelessly inadequate care. If her temperature was below 104 degrees she was given a note entitling her to receive one aspirin tablet on the following day. A woman standing beside me told me that she had become ill on Wednesday, and after waiting outside for three hours was given a note for medicine. The next day she went to fetch it, but there was an air-raid alert at the time that medicines were to have been dispensed. No one was then allowed on the street. Friday, she came one minute too late; Saturday, there was another alert; Sunday, the *Revier* was closed. Monday, she finally reached the table in the hall where the note was to be presented, and learned that there were no more medicines available. She had to wait until there was a new supply.

Betsie looked very sick. A Dutch nurse suddenly came to us and led us up to the front. A few minutes later Betsie was admitted. The sick had to walk past a nurse who distributed thermometers, and each one took her own temperature, standing. If it was high enough, she was sent to the doctor's room. Betsie's was over a hundred and four, and she was considered sick enough for the *Revier*. But she had to wait for the rest of them, in order to go together to Barracks 10, where she would be taken care of.

"How kind the Lord is in taking such good care of me! I had to stand outside such a little while. How the Savior does lead me step by step!" said Betsie.

She was always thankful. My own thoughts were: "This camp is bad enough when one is well; for one who is ill it is altogether dreadful. When, oh, when will there be an end to this?"

As Betsie was being directed to her bed by an unfriendly nurse I was sent away; I should not have come with her at all.

The following day I climbed through a window into the washroom of Barracks 10 and waited there until I had gathered enough courage to go into the hospital.

I found Betsie lying on a narrow cot with a French girl. She was very happy to see me, but told me that the French girl kicked her constantly until she fell out of bed. During the night it had been very bad.

"There is such darkness in the heart of that poor French child," said Betsie. "I told her now and again about the love of the Savior. Jesus is victor; He will conquer this difficulty also. It is not an accident that I have to sleep with this girl."

I asked her if she saw much misery. But, as was so often the case with Betsie, she seemed to see little or nothing of the wretchedness around her. She received no care and no medicine, but was perfectly satisfied.

A nurse came up to me and asked how I had got in. "If I see you here once more, I shall report you."

How very cruel, not even to be allowed to visit my own sick sister.

"There will be an end to this also," I comforted myself, but it was a dark day for me. I missed Betsie more than I could express. Her cheerful animation had always buoyed me up. It was a dismally cold and foggy day, with not a sign of the sun. Walking about outside, I felt rebellion against God rising in my heart.

"Oh, why dost Thou leave us in prison this long while? Why must Betsie suffer so and I may not even visit her? Why should that horrid French child kick her out of bed? Wilt Thou never save us?" Then the Lord spoke to me. I heard three words: *"Rempli de tendresse."*

I stopped and looked around me. There was no one in sight. No, it was the Lord who had spoken these words. I felt deeply ashamed; tears of sorrow filled my eyes, but tears also of gratitude for the wonderful sense of comfort. Oh, I had deserved to be cast off by the Lord. How did I dare to rebel against Him, who so constantly led me, comforted and sustained me? But instead of turning from me, He spoke of His love for me. For me, His rebellious child, He opened His arms wide and said: "Filled with tenderness."

No, I was not alone, and I knew that to those who love God all things work together for good.

A Friendly Old Lady

After three days Betsie came back. But she was still sick, and when she had to appear for roll call at 4:30 next morning she could hardly hold out. She was unable to stand but sat on a stool given to her by an old woman who had risen in the night to bring two stools outside. She had hidden them at the back of the barracks, and this morning appeared triumphantly carrying them to roll call. She gave one to Betsie.

Seeing her laboriously carrying the stools, I asked, "Aren't they much too heavy for you?"

"It is the only thing I can still do for others," she answered.

There was egoism in Ravensbruck, but also love and self-sacrifice. That was the Ravensbruck that revitalized.

Longing

After general roll call at 4:30 A.M. the work commandos had to fall in separately. It was bad not to be enrolled in any particular commando, for the labor pool was a slave market where laborers were sought every morning for the heaviest work. Many women who normally could not have endured the thought of being slaves now seemed to accept their slavery as a matter of fact. The Hollanders, as far as I could see, fortunately did not react in that way. We who were in the knitting commando were assigned to a spot in a far corner of the area behind the row of barracks. Bare walls and a tangle of barbed wire gave it a real prison atmosphere. Before we formed into ranks there was usually a little time to walk back and forth. We stamped on the ground to warm our feet, and walked as briskly as possible. We always met many friends at this time.

"Have you heard any news?"

"Yes, an S.S. said that the queen and the prince were now back in Holland."

Wonderful! That meant they were free at home. What a comfort that was! We would soon return to our fatherland also. We were greatly encouraged; the war could not last much longer. We did not know then that all these optimistic reports were just so many lies, and that only a very small portion of our poor land had been liberated. It was November 1944.

I was daydreaming. In my imagination I saw crowds of people lining the streets. The queen was coming. Slowly she passed by. How we loved her! How she had suffered, with us and for us! I heard Father's calm voice praying for her: "Bless our queen."

Father had prayed for her at the table every day for as many years as I could remember. And during these last years—"bring her back to us speedily." He had not lived to see his prayer answered, but was seeing still more glorious revelations in heaven.

I heard the children singing on the Grote Markt: "Every boy is standing guard for Queen and Fatherland." In the background I saw the Grote Kerk; on the balcony of the town hall stood the queen. Haarlem was free, and the queen had returned.

"*Schneller, aber schneller!*" screamed a *Lagerpolizei*, her strap flicking my coat. It did not hurt me, but I winced from a searing pain, worse than that of physical suffering. I was supporting Betsie, who was about to collapse from being driven so rapidly along that dark wall, and prayed silently: "O Lord, deliver us quickly, and let us share in the joy of our liberated fatherland."

I yearned for freedom! "Someday," I thought, "we shall be free; someday the time will come when we shall no longer be surrounded by electrified barbed wire and prison walls. Wicked women will no longer scream at us, '*Schneller, aber schneller!*' We shall no longer be in the clutches of people trained in cruelty. Someday we shall again see colors, many colors. We shall walk freely wherever we will. Trees, flowers, grass and meadows will again surround us. We shall sing and hear music. We shall not be driven along with whips.

"Someday . . . then, oh, then, how shall it be!"

The earth is a concentration camp. Someday we shall be free. Someday the limitations of earth shall pass away and heaven will be our dwelling place. We shall no longer be conscious of the presence of demons.

Mourning

"To them who belong to the Savior, death is not a pit into which they fall but a tunnel through which they pass into the glorious light of heaven." As I spoke these words I looked at the sad faces about me. Only a little light reached them through the broken window, but I could read the grief in their eyes. Another one of us had passed away. Two had died the day before. Who would be left? Who would ever reach the Netherlands?

"The purpose of our lives does not lie in the brief span of time between our birth and our death. Heaven is our destination. Our friends have arrived there before us; for them it means only glory." Afterwards we sang: "In sweet communion, Lord, with Thee."

Oh, if only I myself could always see things from that point of view. It was such a dark day. Outside it was raining dismally. The last two windowpanes had been broken by the occupants of the upper beds, who had to feel around for the window sill as they climbed down. It was too cold to leave the window open, so we hung cloth over it; but now the room was dark all day. And the only place we could stay was on our narrow beds—two people on a $27\,^1/_2$-inch cot.

The Midwife

Revier 1, the gray hospital barracks, was a cruel center of medical knavery. And there, among the most infamous rascals, lived an innocent and energetic woman, our midwife, who was also a fellow prisoner. All pregnant women whose time had come were brought to her. Occasionally, however, deliveries took place right in the barracks, among all the other women, and without any skilled assistance! But here, too, she helped loyally, lovingly, and what is more, gladly. She had the ability to ignore her surroundings completely and to concentrate exclusively on the ever-amazing miracle of birth.

All she saw was a mother and a tiny, newly-born human being. It did not occur to her that they were despised prisoners, that no father was present to share in the anxiety and the joy attending birth, or that the mother would soon be outside for roll call, sitting on a stool with her back against another prisoner for support, and that there she would nurse her child in the cold nights or the gray morning rains. It did not occur to her that the child, when old enough to hear and interpret sounds, would hear the hoarse, screaming voices and understand the snarling and growling of overwrought women.

During the brief period when the mother was in the care of the midwife, she was treated like an ordinary human being. Her confinement took place under skilled and friendly direction. The first sounds of the newborn child were just as touching as in any nursery in a free land. The feeding of the child was carefully regulated and the mother well cared for. But very soon the mother would again be just a number. She would stand submissively in the cold, during roll call, staring fixedly into space, just one among thousands. She would sleep again in her cramped and dirty bed, but now with the baby beside her. The cry, "*Schwangeren Nachkelle*"[35] would no longer mean for her that welcome additional snack after the meager menu of the day (Leftover food was divided among the pregnant women).

The midwife did not see the screaming guards or see the gray barracks and black streets. She did not see out in the snow the frozen bodies of those who had succumbed before they were admitted to the hospital barracks. She did not see the women standing naked, waiting meekly for a medical examination. The midwife saw a mother and her child. Was she dreaming of the day of liberation? I wondered. In her own way she was marking out the difficult lesson taught by life in a concentration camp.

I marveled at the midwife of Ravensbruck.

Lony

Our barracks had been originally intended to house four hundred people. It now sheltered approximately fourteen hundred. The women prisoners from many concentration camps and prisons were being evacuated to Ravensbruck. *Neue Zugaenge*, new arrivals, were a sad picture. They were often barefooted, always dead tired, at times despairing, and sometimes resigned. Thinly clad, they stood for hours and hours in front of the quarantine barracks.

The stream of newcomers filled our camp beyond its capacity. But this overcrowding had one advantageous result—a lack of adequate supervision. We could go on calmly and uninterruptedly with our daily Bible discussions. Protestants and Catholics, religious trends of all sorts, were gathered in harmony, one in our misery but also one in Christ. There would be no separate Protestant or Catholic areas in heaven. Why should there be here? There was something of heaven in this unity.

One day in late November we were startled by the arrival of two new supervisors in our barracks. One was our new *Aufseherin*. On the day of her arrival she beat a woman so cruelly that she died the following day in the hospital. The other was an additional *Stube-älteste*, named Lony, who walked about with a strap in her hand and used it on the slightest pretext. We felt that these women were a serious threat to our welfare, and decided to start a campaign of prayer for our protection. The following day I went to our customary place back in the barracks for our Bible discussion. Someone whispered to me that Lony was sitting in a dark corner behind me.

"We cannot go on with our meeting today," said someone.

With a few others, I prayed for protection and for guidance, and the Lord clearly directed us to go on as usual. I explained a portion of Scripture and offered a prayer of thanksgiving; and we closed by singing together, "Commit thy ways unto the Lord."

Out of the darkness in the corner came the voice of Lony, "*Noch solch ein Lied!*" (Sing another song like that!) What could this mean? Had she been touched by the singing or was there something else? We sang another song and again came the command, "*Noch solch ein Psalm!*" (Sing another Psalm!)

That day we sang more and longer than ever before. The Lord had answered our prayer above and beyond measure. Not only had the danger of Lony's prohibiting our meetings been averted, she actually wanted a part in them. She understood the Dutch language because she had kept company with a Hollander. As a matter of fact, that was the reason for her being in a concentration camp.

The next day Betsie went to call her. She was standing beside the stove and thought that Betsie had come to warm herself. No despised prisoner was permitted to approach the stove, and Lony seized a blazing piece of wood to drive her away.

"No, I have not come to warm myself, but to invite you to our meeting," said Betsie.

"I haven't the time today," said she, but threw the wood back into the fire.

The next day I invited her. "Oh, woman," she snapped, "leave me alone."

That evening I had a talk with her. What a tragic specimen of humanity she was—what a desperate and despairing creature! At home she ran a brothel, and she herself had a dissipated body and a demoralized soul. I spoke to her of the love of the Savior for sinners and of the judgment that was to come for those who reject Him and continue in sin.

"Now you are a curse to us, but the Lord Jesus can make you a blessing, if only you give your heart to Him."

"*Ach*," said Lony, "such things are impossible in Ravensbruck. This is a hell."

"Yes," I replied, "I too have come to the awful conclusion that this is a hell; but do you know that the greatest danger here is that you will lose your soul to the devil who reigns in this place? And even though it looks as if he were master here, Jesus is nevertheless the conqueror; if you belong to Him you are safe, even here. I know that to be true, for I am calm and happy here, in spite of everything, because I am His child. Repent, Lony, while there is still time."

She actually let me finish what I was saying, but made no further reply. I had a few more such encounters with her, and her attitude did change to some extent. But as long as I was in Ravensbruck she did not come to conversion. I know, however, that God's Word does not return unto Him void. Eternity will reveal whether our talks have borne any fruit or not.

Memorial Service for the Dead

Two women from Vught had passed away. Standing in the entrance of the sleeping room I spoke a few sentences of brief commemoration. On one of the beds lay The Snake, our *Stubeälteste*. Everyone was absolutely quiet as I spoke. Even the Poles, who could not understand what I was saying but who had been told by one of their own number that we were having a memorial service for the dead, were silent and reverent. Suddenly The Snake shouted at me to stop. She was furious. I went on speaking quietly of the faith and courage of the dead, and of the urgent need of repentance when every hour was taking its toll of dead. I bore witness to Jesus, the conqueror of death. Every nerve in my body was taut. Such moments revealed clearly the depths of our suffering, and the constant peril in which we lived. I heard myself speaking calmly, and through it all the hysterical screaming of The Snake as she continued to shout at me. I was not afraid, but I was deeply conscious of the fact that two spheres were in conflict at that moment. It seemed to be something taking place outside myself. Then The Snake jumped up from her bed, seized a whip and rushed at me.

"May I ask you all to remember the dead in a moment of reverent silence?" I heard myself saying. I closed my eyes, expecting the blows to fall, but the silence remained unbroken. As I walked back to my bed I saw The Snake sitting on the edge of her cot. She was still holding the whip, and staring fixedly before her.

Typhus

Typhus had broken out in the barracks opposite ours. Hundreds of women lived there, crowded together, and now they were not allowed to leave the building. They lay, or sat, in endless rows, two or three to each narrow, dirty bed. The quarantine would last for six weeks, and in all that time they would not be allowed outside. Typhus usually runs its course very rapidly, often terminating in a few days—at times, in a few hours. Now and then we would see someone collapse on the *Lagerstrasse*—dead.

Blankets could not be aired or shaken out in that barracks, and the lice that carried the disease multiplied by the hour. More than a thousand women would throng the eight toilets. Clothes were washed under a tap and dried above the beds, where they were reinfected before they were even dry.

Would anyone come out alive from that pool of contagion? I knew that drastic measures would be taken if the disease spread. According to Nazism, mass murder might be necessary in the interest of public health.

Sitting in the window of the barracks was a lovely young woman, holding a small boy on her lap. He was playing with her long braids. Above his head the mother was staring into the distance.

Timidity

Mrs. Bruins, who had tried to defend herself when she was beaten some time ago, had been reported, and was now summoned for a hearing. Her charge was—attacking and striking an *Aufseherin*. I had been present at the time, and now she wanted me to accompany her and explain what had happened. She herself was unable to speak a word of the German language.

My German was fairly fluent, and I agreed to accompany her immediately, although I did feel some reluctance and no little concern. I would have to plead for her before people in whom there was not a semblance of justice, before stupid and cruel officers and *Aufseherinnen*, sadists, who had been methodically trained to torture people, and who kept in practice by daily exercise. But I was not admitted. Mrs. Bruins had to go in alone, and I felt relieved. What little courage I had! And this was not the first time I had observed cowardice in myself. If I had been a brave woman I would have ignored danger and have leaped to the defense of anyone who was being oppressed; I would have pleaded, I would have convinced, I would have . . . I would very often have been opposed, and most of the time it would have been futile. But if I had succeeded only once in pleading and winning a case, it would have been well worth the difficulty and the misery.

But I was not brave. I was often like a timid, fluttering bird, looking for a hiding place. As I pulled my dirty blanket over me

I pressed close to Betsie and cried, softly, so she would not hear me, "Coward and wayward and weak, I change with the changing sky; today so eager and brave, tomorrow not caring to live. But *He* never gives in, and we two will win, Jesus and I."

Hate

"Are all Hollanders so strong, so calm and so controlled, and yet so full of hate?" asked a Russian woman.

I was startled. Was there so much hate among us? I knew, of course, that one of the worst things that Germany had done to us was that it had taught our people to hate. I searched my own heart, but, no, that was not one of my problems. The Lord had given me so much tender care and love that hatred was no temptation to me. His love filled my heart, and where love reigns there is no room for hate. I saw the faults of the German people and the horrors of the present regimes more clearly, and felt them more keenly, perhaps, than many others. I suffered daily from their effects on my person. On the other hand, I had never before so learned to know the Lord Jesus as a tender, loving friend, who never forsakes us or casts us off when we are bad, but rather helps us to gain the mastery over sin. In the foreground of my life there was hardheartedness, savage cruelty, dismal melancholy and darkness; but behind it all I saw my Savior, His arms outstretched, and His face shining with light and love. Therefore I could not hate.

A Multitude of People

Thousands of women were standing in ranks according to barracks, women from all the countries of Europe, from all classes and social strata, and of all ages. Most of them were political prisoners, but there were also many among them who had been sentenced for murder, robbery or other crimes. All of them had been forced to leave their homes, their families and their positions in life to become slaves in Ravensbruck. Most of them had apparently accepted their enforced stay here. Dull resignation was legibly written on their faces.

When the siren wailed, everyone joined her own work commando. There was such a milling around it seemed that thousands had suddenly been added to the throng. I tried to fight my way against the current, but felt it was a power against which I had no resistance. It was a sea of prisoners, of striped dresses and caps. Had there ever before in history been such a vast assemblage of forlorn and wretched creatures?

I escaped to our own barracks. Even here in our beds we were never really alone. To the left and the right of us, behind, before, and above us, everywhere were prisoners. But it was much better here. We had many friends around us. I felt their grief more intensely than the sufferings of the thousands outside, but I could bring a message of comfort to those around me. Now and then I would see a face light up as we spoke of the joyful gospel of Jesus Christ.

I thought back to my cell in Scheveningen. Would I care to go back to it? I didn't know. There were times when I longed very much to be alone, even for an hour or two.

Betsie said to me at one time, "I am beginning to love the multitude."

Was she, perhaps, ripening for heaven? Peace and serenity shone in her face; people were comforted just by looking at her.

The Lost Sheep

The beds above us were occupied by several members of the Red-light Commando, the whores. Some of them were pregnant. These women were usually given the preference when *Tisch-ältesten* were selected, that is, those who were responsible for receiving and dividing the food (with the exception of soup) for forty people. Some of them were indescribably filthy. Our food was usually taken to their beds, and our bread, butter, and sausage divided on their dirty blankets. Once a week we were given butter and sausage. On that morning I would awaken and think, "Mm, good; today we'll have sausage." We were given only one-half of a thin slice, but it was appetizing, and we stretched it sparingly to cover many sandwiches.

As I conducted the Bible discussions these women would often listen from a distance. They were too ashamed to join us. I had often invited them, but without success. Then I tried personal contact, and continued to talk to several of them. Sheer wretchedness made some of them long for a change in their lives.

"When I get back to Holland," said they, "I'm going to begin a new life."

We talked about Jesus, who loves sinners, and who bore their sins also on the cross, and who would help them to live better lives. But we emphasized the fact that conversion, genuine conversion, was necessary. "Half-way measures are of no value." They understood that, too. But for them it was a tremendous step, a plunge into the dark; and many of them were afraid to take it.

Three of these young women were sentenced to the guardhouse. They had received jewels and watches from Jews who had come into the camp and who had succeeded in getting these things into the hands of the women before they had to surrender all their possessions.

The contacts between these women and ourselves had consisted so far of only short conversations at evening roll call. But now the women of our barracks were assembled in front of the guardhouse fence, and the girls were standing like caged animals just inside the bars. One of them called out, "Tante Betsie,[36] are you there?"

"Yes, of course, here I am. How are things going?" answered Betsie.

"Badly; we have to work so hard. It's awful here, and we're so homesick. If only we were back in the barracks with you. That would be a relief."

"The Lord Jesus is everywhere, with you also. You know what He asks of you."

A *Lagerpolizei* put an end to our conversation and drove the girls away from the fence.

We were happy that we had been able to establish contact with these fragments of human flotsam. I had been trying to interest our recent converts in them, but found the same lack of mercy and love for fellow sinners which I had observed before in others.

We political prisoners were all in this penal camp because of the good we had done. We were being innocently oppressed. Because of that fact we were liable to think of ourselves as good people. It was true that we had done no wrong to our fellowmen or to our country. Quite the contrary—that was the very reason we were here. Nevertheless, we were, and are, sinners. We realize that fully when we judge ourselves according to God's holy laws. We are saved only by grace, by forgiveness of our sins. That was perfectly clear to me. But so many of my fellow prisoners were religiously uninformed, and I felt it a great responsibility and burden on my soul. I comforted myself with the thought that the Spirit of God would govern the outcome. He would "convict the world of sin, and of righteousness, and of judgment" (John 16:8, NKJV) I could go on working in complete dependence on Him, and God's kingdom would come in spite of the imperfections of our efforts. God's strength is made perfect in our weakness.

In the Throng

During certain hours of the day there was always a crowd of several hundreds of people in the *Stube*, or anteroom, of the barracks. Food was brought there and distributed, and everyone who entered or left the barracks had to pass through the same room. During peak hours there was a press of people moving in opposite directions. It was fortunate that the atmosphere of our barracks was more good-natured and tolerant than the others. We tried to get through without too much shoving or colliding with others. Our contacts with one another, however, were much too close for comfort. We often found, after we had made our way through the crowd, that there were lice on our clothing. Hollanders from other barracks were hesitant about visiting Barracks 28 for this reason. I always dreaded going through the *Stube* myself, and longed even more fervently for home at such moments.

One day I was struggling to get through the crowd. A work commando had come in late, and was pressing around the *kubel* in which the soup was kept. These *kubels* were really ingenious food-buckets made on the same principle as thermos bottles. They kept the soup boiling hot. The women who had gone to fetch the bread were also just coming in, their arms filled with broad black loaves which they piled up on the floor against the wall. In a corner of the room was a table on which a small supply of medicines was laid out. A nurse was sitting beside it, treating the sad parade that passed before her. She had a practice larger than that of many a city doctor. The sick were standing in line; those with wounds had removed their bandages, and I saw some ghastly sights. The nurse was a Hollander, a kind-looking woman who helped her patients in a friendly manner. She looked tired that day, and no wonder, with such a line of misery passing by. To some of them she gave homemade *norit*—charcoal which she herself had charred and powdered. On the stove was a large pan of some sort of tea which she gave to those with the more serious intestinal disturbances.

The room was large, but more than half of it was taken up by beds, built all the way to the ceiling. And every one of them was occupied. Some of the women were knitting; most of them were staring idly into space. I wondered if they were not disturbed by the turmoil around them. It must have been awful to live in the midst of such a crowd.

I was making my way carefully through the mass of people when a young woman bumped into me. She was an acquaintance, and I asked, "How are you?"

We were standing face to face, looking at each other, and in her eyes was a world of despair. "Annie, don't look like that. Are things so bad?"

"I cannot stand it any longer. If I have to stay in this hell for one more week, I shall go to pieces."

But she would have to stay. God does not ask what we can, or cannot, bear. I took her hand and began to talk to her. "You must not despair, Annie. Jesus is victor, even if you cannot see it. If you are His you will be given strength to go on. He will make you see things from God's point of view, and then you will be strong."

"But what can I do?"

"Surrender yourself to Him. Don't you see that He is standing with arms outstretched; don't you hear Him say, 'Come unto Me'?"

"I would like to very much, but I cannot pray. You pray for me."

Then we prayed. We held each other's hands and had our eyes open. No one who saw us standing there could see that we were praying. All around us was the milling crowd of hundreds of people. When Annie moved on there was an expression of peace on her face. The Lord had heard our prayer.

A Promise

At night, as we walked to the place of roll call, Betsie and I would pray together. It was a walking with God. All around were darkened barracks. And all around were rows of prisoners forming into ranks. Above us spread the starry heavens. We spoke, and then listened for the answer.

How wonderful it will be in heaven, where we shall hear clearly. Now our sin-marred ears make frequent mistakes; our hearing is often distorted. But it was wonderful to listen, and it was such a great comfort. That night the Lord made me a promise: "Before the onset of severe cold you will be free."

Weeks ago He had asked me, when I pleaded that it might not turn cold: "If I ask this sacrifice of you, will you not also bear the cold?" I was so afraid of the cold.

At that time I prayed for strength to endure this also. And now there came this wonderful promise. A little later, at our Bible discussion, I comforted the others. "Before severe cold sets in we shall be released." But I was mistaken. All the prisoners were not to be released until the following spring. The promise had been meant for me alone.

To a Better Fatherland

It was the week before Christmas; Betsie was now seriously ill. She was strangely lethargic and her speech was labored. She had become emaciated in just a few days' time. Her symptoms frightened me, for I had seen them in the women about us. They always ended in death. As I helped her put on her shoes to report for roll call, I noticed that her legs were paralyzed. I then went to the *Block-älteste* and asked if Betsie might not remain behind, but she said: "The commander has ordered that even the dying must report for roll call."

Mien and I carried her through the dark night and supported her as she sat on a small stool. Was she going to die? When I mentioned the possibility, she said hopefully, "That's out of the question; we are going back to the Netherlands together; we shall still do a great many things for others."

She was not afraid to die. She always talked about heaven as if she had already been there. She knew that her life was hidden with Christ in God.

Later in the day I could see that her face was changing. She was deathly ill. It was hard to nurse her on the narrow bed we shared. The lack of cleanliness troubled me more than ever, though I did not believe that Betsie was at all conscious of it. I tried to warm her hands and feet, but observed that mine only grew colder for it. If only I could give her something warm to drink! Never before had I felt our poverty and wretchedness so keenly.

The next morning we again carried her out of the room, but Lony came to meet us. "This is too bad," she said. "Lay her on one of the beds and we'll take her to the hospital after roll call." She actually arranged for a stretcher. Just as we had laid Betsie on it, a Polish woman came by. Seeing us, she knelt down beside the stretcher, made the sign of the cross, and prayed. With tears in her eyes she went on. That was the farewell of the Polish women to whom Betsie had meant so much. Then the sad procession moved toward the hospital.

Sleet stung us as we reached the outside. I stepped close to the stretcher to form a shield for Betsie. We walked past the waiting line of sick people, through the door and into a large ward. They placed the stretcher on the floor and I leaned down to make out Betsie's words.

". . . must tell people what we have learned here. We must tell them that there is no pit so deep that He is not deeper still. They will listen to us, Corrie, because we have been here."

I stared at her wasted form. "But when will all this happen, Betsie?"

"Now. Right away. Oh, very soon! By the first of the year, Corrie, we will be out of prison!"

A nurse had caught sight of me. I backed to the door of the room and watched as they placed Betsie on a narrow cot close to the window. I ran around to the outside of the building. At last Betsie caught sight of me; we exchanged smiles and soundless words until one of the camp police shouted at me to move along.

That noon I was able to call on her. She was full of courage, and assured me that she believed we were to return together. "We are both going back to the Netherlands," said she, and as I was sent away by a nurse she called after me as her final greeting, "Remember now, both of us."

Next morning after roll call, I walked along the side of the hospital barracks where Betsie was lying. I was not too worried about her condition, because she herself had been so very sure that she would get well. Hopefully I looked through the window next to her bed, and there I saw two nurses, holding a sheet by its four corners and lifting a body from the bed. It was completely emaciated, like a skeleton. It was Betsie.

"She is dead," I moaned.

A great loneliness filled my heart. Alone! Alone in Ravensbruck! No more of those wonderfully encouraging conversations, no longer that lively spirit and that childlike faith to buoy me up! But suddenly a sense of peace came over me; yes, more than that, a feeling of sheer joy: "The LORD gave, and the LORD hath taken away; blessed be the name of the LORD" (Job 1:21). Was it God's Spirit speaking within me?

I went to the washroom, where the dead were laid out. There I saw eleven bodies lying on the floor. People who wanted to wash had to step over them. The regime had no respect for the dead.

I fled from the room. A few minutes later, however, I returned and then I saw the face of Betsie, full of peace, and happy as a child. She looked incredibly young. The care lines, the grief lines, the deep hollows of hunger and disease were simply gone. In front of me was the Betsie of Haarlem. It was a bit of heaven in the midst of the surrounding hell. I saw how blessed she was and thought of her present state of happiness. Joy flooded my soul and remained there, triumphant over the grief of my loss. At a memorial service that day I spoke on I Corinthians 15.

How they loved Betsie, these people to whom I was speaking! And what a sorrow this was for us all! Lily, who was in the hospital, tried to come to me, but was not allowed to enter the barracks. She then came to the window, and as I looked into her eyes I was reminded of a wounded animal.

How dark and burdensome days can be! My soul was the battleground of a struggle between light and darkness. Would joy for Betsie's release, or grief for my own loss, win the battle? I prayed:

Teach me, Lord, to bear the burden,
  In this dark and weary day.
Let me not complain to others
  Of a hard and lonely way.

Every storm to Thee is subject,
  Storms of earth, or mind and heart.
Only to Thy will submitting
  Can to me Thy peace impart.

So to suffer, so keep silence,
  So be yielded to Thy will.
So in weakness learn Thy power—
  Teach me, Father, teach me still.

Marusha

Going to bed that evening, I saw a Russian woman looking hopelessly about for a place to sleep. Everyone turned her away unkindly, and a hunted look came into her eyes. How awful to be in prison and not to have a place to sleep! Betsie's place beside me was vacant. I motioned to the woman and threw back the blanket for her. She crept in gratefully and stretched out beside me. She was a bright-looking woman, and as she laid her head on the pillow so close to me I felt a desire to speak to her. But I did not know her language. So I said "*Jesoes Christoes?*" And at once she made the sign of the cross, threw her arms about me and kissed me.

She who had been my sister for fifty-two years, with whom I had shared so much of weal and woe, had left me. A Russian woman now claimed my love; and there would be others too who would be my sisters and brothers in Christ. I wondered if the Lord would provide further opportunities for me to give others the love and care that Father and Betsie no longer needed.

The Missing One

Two days after Betsie's death we were subjected to a *strafappèl* (a disciplinary roll call). One of the fourteen hundred women in our barracks had failed to appear for roll call. It was a Sunday morning, and we had to stand outside from 5:30 until noon. It was cold, but the sunrise was beautiful. The beauty of the sky colored our entire surroundings. We were in good spirits and told each other that it was really not bad. But my legs and feet were swelling dangerously. In every adverse circumstance I now felt a background of comfort in Betsie's passing into glory. She no longer had to stand at roll call; they could no longer punish her.

The women were counted and counted again, then checked off one by one in the *Aufseherin's* record book. That disclosed the name of the missing woman who was the cause of this cruel, collective punishment. They found her, a little Polish woman, lying dead in her bed. We had been punished for the absence of a dead woman. Five of us, including myself, became ill because of that *appèl*. What it was I did not know. We grew thinner and more wasted each day. Inside of ten days the other four women were dead.

After the *strafappèl* one of the girls who was in the guardhouse called out to me, "How are you, Tante Kees?"[37]

The day before she had called, "Tante Betsie, are you there?"

"Tante Betsie died yesterday."

We heard her sobbing. Betsie was loved by the three standing there behind the bars. Now I replied, "I am fine. I am very much comforted and thankful that Tante Betsie is really at home in heaven. How are all of you?"

"Fine. We have all three been converted."

How wonderful! I did not overrate such a remark, but it meant a great deal. It meant, at least, a new beginning. There would still be a battle, but Jesus is the victor. "O Lord, will You continue to work in them through Your Spirit, and forbid that this be only a transient emotion."

Released from Ravensbruck

It was the following morning when over the loudspeaker during roll call came the words: "Ten Boom, Cornelia!"

For an instant I stood stupidly where I was. I had been Prisoner 66730 for so long that I almost failed to react to my name. I walked forward.

"Stand to the side!"

What was going to happen? Why had I been singled out? Had someone reported the Bible?

The roll call dragged on. From where I stood I could see almost the entire *Lagerstrasse*, tens of thousands of women stretching out of sight, their breath hanging white in the night air.

When the siren sounded to signal the end of roll call, the *Block-älteste* took me by the arm. She was unusually friendly. I had known her as a hard woman, with cruel eyes and an erect, military figure. She now asked me how long I had been a prisoner, and brought me to the camp square. We were joined by a few Germans and one Dutch prisoner, and together we went to the administration barracks and stood in line.

An officer seated behind a large desk stamped a paper and handed it to the woman in front of him.

"*Entlassen!*" he said.

Entlassen? Released? Was—was the woman free then? Was this—were we all—

He called a name and another prisoner stepped to the desk. A signature, a stamp:

"*Entlassen!*"

At last "Ten Boom, Cornelia," was called. I stepped to the desk, steadying myself against it. He wrote, brought down the stamp, and then I was holding it in my hand: a piece of paper with my name and birthdate on it, and across the top in large black letters: CERTIFICATE OF DISCHARGE.

Dazed, I followed the others through a door at our left. There at another desk I was handed a railway pass entitling me to transportation through Germany to the Dutch border.

"What a Christmas you are having this year!" said a *Lagerpolizei*, and I felt her happiness for me was tinged with a bit of envy. "Well, yes, but you won't get back to your country," said another. "The Netherlands is free" (not so, I learned later); "you won't be able to get across the border."

Entlassen! But first, another parade of nakedness before a doctor. Such humiliation! The insolent face of that wretched creature, looking me up and down with scornful disdain. "Oedema," was his verdict. "Hospital."

I could thank the *strafappèl* of the previous day for my swollen feet, but prisoners had to be released in good condition. I would have to sign a statement on leaving the camp that I had never been ill and had never had an accident.

In the Hospital Barracks

Reporting at the hospital that noon, I was admitted and was then kept waiting in the *Stube*. In it was a large table against the window and double-decked beds on all sides. All of the beds were filled with patients, seriously ill. On the table lay a patient. A doctor and four nurses were working over her. She was suffering dreadfully and screaming horribly. It seemed to go on for hours.

A woman who could scarcely walk came out of the large ward. She had on only a shirt, and was as thin as a skeleton. Her bare legs tottered and she begged for help, but someone called out to her that she could very well walk alone. There was an expression of unspeakable agony on her emaciated face; her eyes were bulging with terror. Her clawlike hands reached out for the table. Had I come into a hell? My eyes seemed glued to the horrible scene. The screaming of the woman on the table cut through my soul. I tried to close my eyes and ears, but could not. Was this all an evil nightmare? Then I looked around at the many sick women who were also witnessing this scene. Some of them seemed isolated in their own pain; others had the desolate look of resignation that could be seen on so many faces in Ravensbruck. And some of them were hard and cold. I knew that these had succumbed to the most dangerous disease of the concentration camp, egoism.

"There will be an end to this also," I said to myself. It was the sop of comfort I always gave myself when things were very bad. It always helped a little, but did not give me the staying power that I needed. "You will not leave my soul in hell," I whispered. "Savior, You have borne our griefs."

A woman with an angry face, my new *Stube-älteste*, ordered me to follow her, and directed me to a bed among those of the eight other discharged prisoners. Some of them had already been here for two months, and were still waiting for a doctor to approve their release. I wondered how long I would have to wait. I had learned to be patient, but this was really difficult. I was lying in my high, narrow bed beside a woman with scabies. Around me were German women, all of whom had been punished because they had been having sexual relationships with foreigners.

The women and girls around me were horrible creatures. In the large ward there were many patients who had been mutilated in the bombardment of a train and brought here for treatment. There were also many who had had serious operations. The suffering was appalling. But if anyone groaned, one of these discharged German prisoners would mimic her. They were incredibly mean and cruel. Their harsh voices threatened, cursed and jeered the whole day long.

That first night I was awakened by patients calling "*Schieber!*" I did not recognize the word at the time, and realized only later that they were calling for bedpans. The seriously ill and wounded patients who were incapable of standing, to say nothing of going to the bitterly cold toilet room, were begging for them. The most seriously ill were usually placed in the lower beds, but at times even in the upper bunks. Some of these patients tried to help themselves down and fell from their high beds to the floor. Perhaps they were already dying; in any case, altogether weakened as they were, they could not hold on tightly enough, and during that one night three patients fell out of their beds and died on the floor.

The second night I spent in this hell I decided to take the bedpan chore upon myself. Then I saw the suffering at close range. I helped one woman who had to lie on her stomach because part of her back and her leg had been shot away. I lifted her carefully. As I helped and encouraged her gently, she asked, "Who are you? You are a good woman. There are only evil women here. Where did you come from?" Just because I treated her with common human decency, I was an exception.

Some of the patients seemed to me to be in plaster casts. But later I realized that their bodies were completely emaciated, nothing but skin over bones, and therefore felt hard to the touch. As I helped them I would tell them about Jesus, a little more each night.

Opposite my bed were two Hungarian gypsies who were indescribably dirty and malicious. One of them had a completely gangrenous foot, which she would at times thrust out of her bed as if she were angrily trying to infect others. In her hand she held the nasty bandage she had removed from her foot. One night the bedpans were nowhere to be found. This woman and a few others had hidden them for their own use, to escape going to the cold toilet room. I begged the women to think of the patients who were seriously ill, and who could not be cared for unless the bedpans were given back to us. But there was no response.

In the middle of the night a French girl discovered that the Hungarian had a bedpan hidden under her blanket. I took it away, and a few minutes later went back to bed. Suddenly I heard the French girl screaming for help. The Hungarian, in revenge, had thrown her filthy bandage over the girl's face. Then she did the same thing to me. In the dark I saw her dirty hand above my face. I flung the bandage to the floor and hurried away to wash.

Back in bed, I was overwhelmed by a sense of loathing and fear. I prayed to the Savior to protect me. I felt so helpless amid all this evil and danger of infection. A little later I fell asleep. Dangers still hovered around me, but I felt safe in the arms of Jesus.

Oelie

On a bed next to the window, diagonally across from me, lay a feebleminded girl. She was about fifteen years of age but had the mental development of an eight-year-old. She was completely emaciated but had a sweet face, gorgeous eyes, and lovely, wavy hair. Her voice was sweet and very touching as she begged for her mother. She was lying in front of the window, and the first night I saw her she frightened me. She had removed the bandage of toilet paper and exposed her back, which had been operated upon. The moon shed a ghastly light over her wasted body. I spoke to her softly, and each evening thereafter I would tell her a little more about the Savior. The last night I asked her what she knew, and then she told me, in her soft, touching voice: "The Lord Jesus loves Oelie, and has borne her punishment on the cross. Now Oelie may go to heaven, and Jesus is there right now, busy preparing a little house for Oelie."

"What is it like in that little house?"

"It is very beautiful. There are no wicked people as in Ravensbruck. There are only good people and angels. And Oelie will see Jesus there."

"When you have pain, what will you do?"

"I will ask Jesus to make me brave, and I will think of the pain that Jesus suffered to show Oelie the way to heaven."

"Shall we thank Him together for what He did for you and me?"

Oelie folded her hands; together we gave thanks, and I knew why I had to spend this dreadful week in Barracks 9.

During the night following my release, I was walking in the hospital corridor and observed that the windows were solidly frosted. The water in the bucket had a thick layer of ice on it. It was the first night of bitter cold, and the temperature was down to twenty below zero.

I no longer had to appear at roll call, that most dreadful of experiences when the weather was cold. I was to be in the hospital a week and would then be free. Now at the time of morning roll call I could hear from my bed the rhythmic stamping of thousands of feet. It continued for an hour and a half as the prisoners stood in the wind. God had saved me eight hours before the onset of severe cold.

Citizenship

There had been some improvement in the treatment of the Hollanders. From the dirtiest barracks, where they had to live with the Polish women, they were now moved to the cleanest one, which they shared with German women. The Polish women were mostly market folk from Warsaw, who were, as a Polish lady told me, the poorest and filthiest inhabitants of Poland. All of the

Hollanders were deloused and placed under the supervision of a more humane *Block-älteste*. The latter did not send them out of the barracks for roll call until it was necessary. That saved them at least an hour of standing outside.

We heard that great changes for the better had also been made in the treatment of Dutch men. What was the cause of these sudden improvements? The rumor running through the camp, with a great deal of credence, was that all Hollanders who had been brought to the camp as political prisoners after the entrance of America into the war had been made honorary citizens of the United States. They were considered as American allies in the war. Naturally, we were happy about it, and hoped it would have an advantageous effect on our treatment during the period of liberation.

I told the story to a dying girl. "I think it is much more important that our citizenship is in heaven through Jesus Christ," said she.

Rechecked

The next day I had to go back to the main hospital for rechecking. I was approved, and now I knew that I was really going to be free. Coming out of the barracks, I looked about me. Was this actually the last time I would look on this somber place, on this bleak and leaden misery? In the snow lay the dead body of a young woman. Her small, delicately shaped hands were folded as if in prayer, her knees drawn up as if she had died in pain. Her sweet face, white as the snow about her, was peaceful; her dark, wavy hair lay like a halo about her head, sharply outlined against the snow. She was elegantly dressed.

What could be her story? I didn't know, but I could tell one thing about its end. She had been sick and had succumbed before she was admitted to the hospital. Many dead were lying in front of the *Revier* these days. At one time this woman had been happy, well cared for, and surrounded by love. Then the waves of this regime had swept her from her moorings and brought her here—a white flower, dead in the blackness of this camp.

Toward Freedom

Friendly prisoners helped us in the dressing room. There were two of us Hollanders. I did not know my companion, a young woman named Claire Prins. She was ill, but fortunately was being released. Eight German girls and women were also being discharged. We were generously provided with clothing. After I was entirely dressed I was given a package containing my own clothes brought from Scheveningen and some of Betsie's besides. Altogether it made quite a heavy pack.

We were kept waiting at the gate, and there someone told me that Mrs. Waard and Mrs. Jansen had just died. That reminded me of an *appèl* of two months ago. Betsie had not stood beside me. The weather was raw and rainy and I asked her afterwards, "How was everything?"

"Fine," said she, "it was a wonderful roll call. Mrs. Waard thanked the Lord with me for His death on the cross for her."

Mrs. Waard had not at first been the least bit interested; she had, in fact, made fun of our Bible discussions. Now she had come to complete surrender. "Promoted to glory," I said to myself.

So I walked out of the gate, comforted and thankful that I had been privileged to testify within these walls to the saving death of Jesus. Yes, even Betsie's death was not too big a price for the eternal salvation of souls. In an office outside the camp we were given back our personal *effekten*: money, and my gold ring and watch. At the same time we were given a warning—we had been told before that we would receive one. This time it was on the subject of the misdemeanor of my German companions.

"Remember now, that you are to live better lives, and no longer give your bodies to foreigners. Your own countrymen are giving their lives at the front. Every German woman and girl is duty bound to place her body at the disposal of any German soldier."

I leaned wearily against a desk. "Haven't you learned to stand yet?" snarled an officer. For the last time I snapped into position.

Was I free at last? The weather was beautiful. Everything was covered with snow. An *Aufseherin* escorted us to the station. We climbed a gentle ascent and looked around us. A large group of "slave" prisoners, sent out to chop wood, were walking between the trees. Driven along by their overseers, they were going to their heavy work. And we, we were walking toward freedom.

On the street we met another group of prisoners who had to build roads and unload potatoes and coal. All of these women and girls would have to go back to camp, while we were going to our own country. A feeling of deep melancholy came into my heart. How much I was leaving behind me—all that endless sea of grief!

The sun was shining on the frozen lake. On the opposite shore we could see Fürstenberg, with its ancient castle and abbey, picturesque against the hills. The sunlight on the snow was reflected in a myriad of spectral colors. The pines, with their heavily laden branches, looked like Christmas trees.

"How Hungry I Am"

We were all taking the train as far as Berlin, where we would go our separate ways. We had each been given enough bread for one day, and ration coupons for three additional days. But somehow, my supply of bread and my packet of ration coupons were either lost or stolen on the very first day, as I waited for the train, and the Germans would sell me nothing without ration coupons. With my undernourished body I would somehow have to get through the next days without food.

At last a train pulled into the station and we crowded eagerly to it, but it was for military personnel only. Late in the afternoon we were allowed aboard a mail train, only to be put off two stops farther on to make room for a food shipment. The trip became a blur. We reached a huge, bomb-gutted terminal in Berlin sometime after midnight.

It was new Year's Day, 1945. Betsie had been right: she and I were out of prison.

Snow drifted down from a shattered skylight as I wandered, confused and frightened, through the cavernous station. I knew that I must find the train to Uelsen, but months of being told what to do had left me robbed of initiative. At last someone directed me to a distant platform. Each step now was agony in the stiff new shoes. When I reached the platform at last, the sign said not Uelsen but Olsztyn, a town in Poland in exactly the opposite direction. I had to cross those acres of concrete floors again.

A train was standing on the track and I climbed aboard. By the time it started up I was dizzy for lack of food. A couple of German girls told me I might be given something to eat at the N.S.F. (National Sozialistisches Frauenwerk, assistance to traveling women and children). And so I asked a friendly Red Cross nurse at the station of a small town, where we had to change trains, if there was an N.S.F. house there. She pointed it out to me, down at the far end of the platform. One of the workers opened the door for me and I told her of my predicament—no food and no coupons.

"Oh, yes, that's an old story," said she, "first use up your coupons and then ask for food. Get out of here before I call the police!" And she slammed the door in my face.

Going back to the Red Cross, I told the nurse what had happened. "Here," said she, "eat this quickly." She shoved a plate of pea soup toward me and stood guard while I ate, lest some superior should happen by. This food was intended only for soldiers. How delicious that soup did taste! There was meat in it. I feasted on it, but felt, at the same time, like a beggar, and looked around apprehensively. Fortunately, there was no one about who should not have seen me greedily bolting this food.

One night Claire and I had to spend an hour or two waiting in a station. As I dozed in an empty coffee bar my head dropped forward until it rested on the small table in front of me. A blow on my ear sent me sprawling almost to the floor.

"This is not a bedroom!" the furious station agent shrieked. "You can't use our tables to sleep on!"

How hard and unfriendly these people were! We were of no use to their war machine; so, really, of what value were we at all? In our good Holland even the smallest child is taught to respect older people; but that was unheard of in the Germany of 1945.

I was to meet charitable people on one more occasion during the trip. At a large station I asked an officer if there was any possibility of getting some food. He looked at us kindly, and motioned to a boy who was driving a motorcart of baggage along the platform. Before we knew what was happening to us we were sitting on the cart and were being given a ride to a small house just outside the station.

Here I took part in a scene that carried me back completely to the genial Germany of pre-war days.

A motherly woman placed bread, delicious jam, and coffee before us, and a pretty girl moved about briskly bringing us everything she could think of. The officer stood by and teased the girl: "And has Greti already telephoned Hans?" he asked. Greti blushed.

The woman urged us to eat and to enjoy ourselves. Speaking about the officer, she said, "He is like a father to us all."

Then the air-raid siren sounded, and we had to hurry away. The trains would not stop here for long because bombs were very frequently dropped at this spot. For a few brief moments I had been in the Germany of former years.

Checking Out

Claire and I reached the German border at Uelsen; we had to stop there before we could enter Holland. Having found the building where the political police were housed, we were received by several Dutch Nazi boys and girls, who invited us to sit down.

One of the girls, a child of about sixteen, perched on the edge of a table in front of us and said, "Well, so you've come out of a concentration camp! I don't suppose you had too jolly a time of it there. Awkward, isn't it, to be a prisoner? It must be pretty nice, seems to me, for you to be free again."

How appallingly ignorant these young people were! I found myself incapable of speech. They evidently had not the slightest conception of the cruelty of the regime with which they had voluntarily associated themselves. I was dead tired, but was happy to get out in the street again, though I had to look a long time for a place to stay. We could have spent the night among the collaborators at the N.S.B. office, but we would have slept in the snow on the streets before going back into that atmosphere of untruth.

Early the next morning we returned to the station. And from there we crossed the border into occupied Holland. We had passed through many ruined cities of Germany, past the rubble of houses where once had lived happy families, who were doubtless now wandering around in search of shelter. What a curse there was upon that country! What an enormous amount of suffering Hitler had brought upon his people!

5

The Fatherland

We were standing in line at the customs shed and the sign of the little station building said *Nieuwerschans*. Claire could scarcely stand straight. Her leg was alarmingly swollen. She felt ill, and I, too, was at the end of my endurance. A man saw our predicament and came toward us. "It's no go with those legs," he said in Dutch. "Suppose you give me that pack." He took Claire by the arm and led us into the customs office. But he finished there before we did and, when we came outside, he was nowhere to be seen. Then two workmen kindly offered their help. "Just walk between us," said they, "and we'll see you safely aboard your train."

We were in Holland! Here there was friendliness and helpfulness. How wonderful to be in our own homeland again! During the trip through Germany I had felt no real joy about my release. Now, I was just beginning to realize it. Now I dared to enjoy it.

The Deaconess Home

The train was going only as far as Groningen, a city in northern Holland. Near the station was a deaconess-run convalescent home. I went directly there and I asked to speak to the superintendent.

"Sister Tavenier cannot come at the moment, for she has to attend a religious service in one of the wards. I'm afraid you will have to wait."

"Could I perhaps attend it also?" I asked.

"Why, of course; I'll fetch you when it starts. You may go into the waiting room meanwhile."

"Nurse, have you anything for me to drink?"

"Yes, but you are ill. I'll bring you some tea and rusk."

A few minutes later she placed it before me, saying, "I have not put butter on it, for you are having intestinal trouble, and dry rusk is better for you."

I felt deeply touched. Here was a woman who was thinking of me and considering what was good for me.

The waiting room was typical of hospital waiting rooms everywhere. On the divan lay a man who had been up all night with his dying wife, and was now resting. A boy sauntered in, the boredom of a convalescent written all over his face. The family of a very sick patient stood whispering together; they were being permitted to visit the sickroom one at a time.

A moment later I was lying in a comfortable chair with my legs outstretched on a bench, and a wonderful feeling of rest descended upon me. I was in the Netherlands, among good people. My suffering was ended.

A nurse came to fetch me. In the ward, chairs had been arranged in a semicircle between the beds, facing a table. An elderly minister walked in and a hymnal was handed to me. I could see the nurses and patients glancing stealthily at me. How neat the beds were, how clean the sheets and pillowcases! And the floor was spotless.

Now the minister was speaking in a well-modulated voice. He read the words of a hymn, which we all joined in singing. I found myself constantly making comparisons: the dirty dormitory, infection-ridden and filthy, the beds full of lice, and then this.

The hoarse voices of the slave drivers, and the mature, melodious voice of Dominee Hoogenraad.

Then we sang. But on this point there was little contrast. We did sing in Ravensbruck, and that would always remain a precious memory. But the background was different here. Here, we were permitted to sing.

As in a Happy Dream

I was sitting in the room of the superintendent.

"Miss Prins has been taken care of, and is already lying in a fresh bed with clean sheets. We shall take good care of her. But now, what must be done with you?"

"I don't know, Sister."

A wonderful feeling of relaxation had come over me. I was surrounded by people, none of whom was angry with me.

"I know what." She touched a bell, and a young nurse entered.

"Sister, take this lady to the nurses' dining room and give her a warm dinner."

The young nurse took my arm, and as we walked down the corridor she asked: "Where are you actually going; where is your home?"

"In Haarlem," I replied.

"Oh, do you know Corrie ten Boom there?"

I looked at her and recognized her as one of our Y.W.C.A. leaders.

"Truus Benes!" I exclaimed, in delight.

"Why, yes, that is my name," said she, "but I don't believe I know you."

"I am Corrie ten Boom."

"Oh, no, that's impossible. I know her very well. I've been at camp with her several times."

"But really, I am she."

We looked at each other and both of us laughed. I had caught a glimpse of myself in a mirror, and understood why she had not recognized me. My face was thin and pale, my mouth wide. My hair fell queerly about my face, and my eyes were hollow. My coat was dirty, for I had at times lain on the floor of the train. The belt was hanging loose; I had not enough energy left to fasten it.

In the dining room we sat opposite each other at a small table, and I asked about our mutual acquaintances. Was Mary Barger still living? Jeanne Blooker and . . . ? It was ridiculous to ask such questions. After all, it had been only a short year since I last heard from them. But what a long, long year it had been!

I ceased my questioning. I was eating—potatoes, Brussels sprouts, meat and gravy, and for dessert, pudding with currant juice and an apple.

"I have never seen anyone eat so intensely," said one of the nurses later. She had been watching me from a nearby table. With every mouthful of food I swallowed I could feel new life streaming into my body. I had once said to Betsie in camp, "When we get home, we shall have to eat carefully, perhaps taking only small amounts of food at a time."

"No," said Betsie, "God will see to it that we shall be able to retain all sorts of food right from the start."

I was not eating lightly. Truus kept putting more on my plate. How wonderfully good that food did taste! I shall remember that meal as long as I live.

Then came a warm bath. They could hardly get me out of it. Just one minute more of that refreshing water around me! My poor, sick skin, damaged by lice, seemed to become softer at once from the wonderful warm water. Coming out of the bath, I felt like a new being.

And then they dressed me. There proved to be several ex-leaders of the Netherlands Girls' Clubs among the nurses, and a couple of them provided my toilette. One of them had lingerie for me, another shoes and a dress and pins for my hair. They dressed me up as if I were a doll. I felt so very happy that I laughed for sheer joy. How sweet they were to me!

These young women had been trained in kindness to others. In that evil place from which I had just come I was in the power of men and women who had been trained in cruelty. Now I was surrounded by love and friendship and care.

I was then taken to a lovely bedroom, the room of one of the nurses who was away on leave. As I lay in bed I looked around. How lovely the combination of colors! I seemed to be starved for color, for my eyes could not gaze enough to satisfy them. My bed was delightfully soft and clean, with thick woolen blankets, light in weight but warm. Tucked under my swollen feet was an extra pillow, placed there by a thoughtful nurse.

On a shelf was a row of books. Outside, I heard the whistle of a boat and children calling to one another; far in the distance was the sound of singing, and then, oh, the chimes of a carillon! I closed my eyes, and tears wet my pillow.

One of the nurses took me to her room, where I heard a radio again for the first time. A record of Gunther Ramin, playing a Bach trio, was being broadcast. The organ tones flowed about and enveloped me.

I sat on the floor beside a chair and sobbed. It was too much joy. I had rarely cried during all those months of suffering. But now I could not control myself. My life had been given back to me as a gift. Harmony, beauty, colors and music. They who have suffered as I did, and have returned, will understand what I mean.

Two mounted police called at the Deaconess Home.

"How are the two prisoners from Germany?"

"Fine, but how did you know that they were prisoners?"

"We saw them at the station, and were sorry that we were not free at the time to help them. But we did follow them until we saw them enter the Deaconess Home. We knew then that they were in good hands. Oh, it was easy to see that they were prisoners, they looked so bad."

In Holland people were interested in caring for the aged and weak. How wonderful it was to be home!

Harmony

I was in church for the first time. A mighty cathedral, with colored windows softening the light, lofty arches and columns, all speaking of centuries of devout tradition. The organ began to play. How wonderfully touching its tones! What harmony there was of color, light and sound, and also the atmosphere of praying people who had gathered to hear about God. Oh, I know they were sinful people with many petty ideas, but how wonderful that they were here! God's love had drawn them to this place.

I was again making comparisons. The gray and black monochrome of barracks and dirty cinder streets; the screaming and scolding, and the moaning of Ravensbruck, a sphere of sadism and suffering. First disharmony, then harmony. The minister read from the Bible, and I listened. My soul was thrilled and lifted heavenward as he prayed.

Home

I was once more at home in the house on the Barteljorisstraat!

Much had been stolen: four oriental rugs, my typewriter and, what was worse, the watches and clocks that had been left at our home for repairs. I also missed certain books. Now why had they been taken? Did the men who had come to arrest me think, perhaps, that there might be valuable papers hidden in them?

But I was not looking for what was missing; I was enjoying the many things that had been left. My piano was still there, Father's painted portrait, the beautiful paintings of Miolee, Father's chair, the antique cupboard, and the buffet in the dining room. Oh, there were many precious things left.

But I was there alone. The two who had lived with me in this house, with whom I had shared such an unusually harmonious life, were no longer there. I stood leaning against Father's bed, thinking about their present happiness. They were seeing the solution of problems more clearly than I could on earth. They were seeing heavenly colors and hearing heavenly music. How richly blest both of them had been in their capacity to enjoy life! That would now be unlimited. And, too, they were now seeing the Savior. They were at home in a much deeper sense than I was, and some day, I, too, would go home.

I was happy. My joy in their happiness shone through the grief of my loss. I dared to be happy. My life had been given back to me, and I would perhaps still have opportunities to help and comfort people. I had been purged and purified, and had learned from experience much that I had only superficially believed before. Persecution, distress, hunger, nakedness; nothing can separate us from the love of God in Christ Jesus. More than conquerors through Christ, also over difficulties yet to come.

Much work, I hoped, lay ahead of me; perhaps loneliness, too. No, not loneliness. I would love others, and then one does not long remain lonely. Our home had always been a hospitable one, and it would continue to be so.

Girl's Club

My senior scout club, The Rangers, was meeting with me for the first time. The young people were sitting all around me. Some of them had pressed my hand in silent emotion; others had enthusiastically slapped me on the shoulder.

"Tante Kees, it's wonderful to have you back!"

What a joy it was to see all those young faces that were now turned toward me with such confidence. They had developed spiritually during the past year. They had met faithfully without me almost every week, though most of them were thin from undernourishment and hard work.

They had become more independent. They had had a hard time, chopping wood, bringing food from distant places and riding bicycles without tires. Things they had never been able to do before they had now learned through hardship. I told them about my experiences.

"If you belong to the Savior you need fear nothing. I have learned that by experience. He is stronger than all temptation. Shall we work together to dispel some of the darkness about us? There is a disrupted Netherlands to be rebuilt. Shall we help in its reconstruction in the strength of Jesus? In Him we shall be more than conquerors."

What a joy it was to lead them! But there were young people everywhere, and opportunities everywhere. I could see in my imagination the *Lagerstrasse*. Roll call had just ended. Before going into the *Siemenscommando* two young girls approached me.

"Tante Kees, give us a message for today."

I repeated for them, "Be thou faithful unto death, and I will give thee a crown for life. Fear not, only believe." A few minutes later they were walking rigidly in step as they marched off to the factory.

As my scout group was leaving, one of them came back and said: "Go with us to the country at Eastertime, won't you? And are you going camping with us this year?"

I answered absentmindedly. My thoughts were with those I had left behind. Ravensbruck was not yet free.

Memorial

New members were being confirmed in the Grote Kerk. The day before, May the 5th, the occupying German forces had surrendered. But they were still in Holland. The Canadians were expected to arrive at any moment. The church was filled to capacity. It was the first service in liberated Haarlem, and I sat in the high pew that had been my place for the past several years. The sun was shining through the stained glass windows, splashing the white walls with color. The organ was playing. Then the congregation sang:

"If God had not stood with us,
And strengthened us to stand,
How soon we would have fallen
And perished from the land."

After the closing prayer we all rose, and there was a moment of absolute silence. We were thinking of those who had died. One minute of silence. Father, Betsie, Piet and so many others. Then the organ started playing the "Wilhelmus," our beloved national anthem. But I could not join in the singing, and there were others like me.

Outside, the Grote Markt was full of flags, and people were streaming out of the church. Suddenly we heard shots. Cars were coming out of the Koningstraat at a furious speed, cars filled with Germans who were shooting right and left into the crowd. We ran into the Smedestraat. Now, what could that mean? We would not be really free until later; the enemy was still in the land.

Shaved Heads

There was shouting in the streets outside my window. A jostling, jigging throng was passing by. There was laughter and blowing of horns, and the singing of "Oranje Boven."[38] I went to the window and looked out. What a crowd of young men on the street! They had suddenly come out of months and even years of hiding underground. What a number of children! Many of the latter had never celebrated the *Oranjefeest* before; some of them had, five years ago, but five years is a long time to a child. What a lot of orange color! Where could it all have come from so quickly?

I had a sudden impulse to join in the fun and to follow the crowd to the Grote Markt. My legs were still not functioning very well, but I leaned on the arm of one of the family.

How crowded the Markt was, and how happy the people were! Germans were still walking around, but they were ignored. They would soon be gone and would do us no more harm. Suddenly everyone hurried in the direction of Stadhuis,[39] and there we saw three girls being dragged up the steps. Several men surrounded them on the stairs. The girls were Hollanders who had had relations with German soldiers. The people around me were laughing, screaming and shouting. In front of the Stadhuis scaffolding had been erected. I couldn't imagine why it was there, but it stood on the same spot as had the scaffold in the dark Middle Ages, and I shivered.

Now I could see the face of one of the girls. Her head had been raggedly shorn, and long strands of hair still hung about her face. But she looked much like the girls in the prison. She was livid with suppressed fury. To me she looked like a backward child. Her face was coarse. Flowers were thrust into her hands, and a boy seized her arm and moved it in time to the singing of "Oranje Boven" by the crowd. Another held flowers over her head, and finally, orange-colored paint was smeared over her bald crown. For a second her eyes met mine, and I felt like crying out to the boys who were tormenting her: "Be careful; you are destroying something!"

An older woman was next dragged to the front. She was wild and tried to defend herself. Her dark eyes glittered fiercely, and the people around me shrieked with laughter. This woman was much more fun than the other, who had submitted passively to being shorn. But she was powerless against the superior strength of her captors, and her head was clipped, as also was the neatly waved head of the next victim, a pretty girl, who submitted in silent fury to the shearing. Someone in the crowd then started to sing the "Wilhelmus," and she, too, had to keep time with them. But this was awful. The "Wilhelmus" was so sacred to me. I turned away. After I reached home I could hear the procession going by. I heard the laughing and screaming, but did not look out.

The girls who were being led past my house were guilty, and I could understand how those who were tormenting them had come to do so. They had been so provoked. They had long borne in silence the humiliating persecution of the men these girls had so easily accepted, and the joy of liberation must have its expression. But this was not the way.

Yet, might it not have been much worse on Holland's Bijltjes dag (hatchet day, or day of reckoning)? I had often thought, with concern, about those who would on that day be the objects of the hate that they themselves were engendering in the hearts of an otherwise peace-loving people. Almost every Hollander had his own personal sorrow, his own experience of humiliation, his own score to settle. How dreadful it would have been if later on he would have had to look back to the day of liberation with shame because of the murder of a fellow man. How did it happen that God restrained the powers of evil on that day? Was it because many hearts were praying? I do believe so. I know that a queen was praying for the Netherlands.

Postlude

I was looking through a beautiful house in a magnificent woods. The fragrance of flowers was being wafted inside through an open window. Birds were singing. I stood at the window for a moment looking out over a field of colors, with patches heavy with bloom. The trees were of varying shades of green. No, this is not a fairy tale I am about to tell; it really happened.

"Have you observed how beautiful the woodwork is?" asked the owner, as she rubbed her hand lovingly over the elegant paneling.

I recalled a dark night in the concentration camp at Ravensbruck. Betsie had awakened me with, "Our house is so elegant that the woodwork is equally beautiful throughout the entire house. And it should be, too, because the people we are going to help will need such an attractive environment that they will forget this dreary camp." Had Betsie been prophetic?

This house would soon be the happy home of people who had been released from the wretchedness of imprisonment. We would work together in the fields, in the woods, in the garden and in the house. There would be singing and playing of good music. This was not to be merely a rest home, but a place of recuperation, where the Netherlands would be rebuilt, where some of its wounds would be healed, and where people would regain their zest for living and working.

Later on, this home would be used for others who had never been in a prison, but who would find healing here. Who? That I did not know, but God would send them to us.

There would be obstacles to overcome. It would take money, a great deal of money, and our country was poor. What should I do for fuel? How should I obtain nourishing food? We would have to begin very soon, and there was still much that we needed. How?

Looking back into the past, I whispered: "Persecution, distress, hunger, nakedness; in all this we are more than conquerors through Him who loved us." Then I prayed, "Lord, I am expecting much from You. Take my hand in Yours and lead me as Your child. Let many souls find You in this home."

I recalled an expression used by my father, "The Lord has led me by a most extraordinary manifestation of Providence." I looked forward to the future, knowing that "Jesus Christ is the same yesterday and today and forever." He had been with me in the valley of the shadows, and if in the future there were to be green pastures and still waters, there, too, would His hand guide me.

In the Kenaupark of Haarlem stood a beautiful tree, a wild cherry. Every spring it bore such a wealth of blossoms that the residents of Haarlem called it "the bride of Haarlem." If one stood under it and looked up he would see a luxuriant canopy of white blossoms. Father would go to see it each spring. Betsie and I would watch the blossoms grow larger and larger, and stand under the tree, arm in arm, when the beauty was at its height. Then for days our morning walk would take us over the carpet of fallen petals.

*In 1968, the Israeli authorities honored Corrie ten Boom as a
Righteous Gentile — planting a tree on the Avenue of the Righteous.*

Now the bride of Haarlem had been chopped down. The
massive trunk had not been too much for even unskilled hands to
lay low in time of need. The people of Haarlem had no fuel with
which to cook their scanty rations, and in their cold and hunger
they did not think of spring beauty or of tradition.

I walked through the Kenaupark, looking for the tree. But it
was gone! And I was walking alone. Betsie, my sister, whom Haarlem had loved, was not at my side. Truly, the bride of Haarlem
had been cut down. Nor was my father's arm linked in mine, for
Haarlem's Grand Old Man had died in a cruel prison.

I looked up. April clouds obscured the sun; but they themselves were radiant with a golden luster that shed a glow over the
earth and touched everything with color.

Clouds, too, can give light if only the sun shines on them.

Notes

Chapter 1

1. Political police (a department of the Gestapo).
2. Aunt Wilhelmina (Mien, nickname)
3. Permit.
4. Soft drink.
5. Trade name for a health biscuit.
6. Coin then equal to about eighty cents.
7. Informer in service of the Nazis.

Chapter 2

8. Madam.
9. Name for the Army in Germany.
10. Bucket (or pail) for sewage disposal.
11. Orderly or Red Cross worker.
12. A female Headguard.
13. Cold food.

Chapter 3

14. A girl from Sarasani's Circus.
15. Cement cells.
16. District Commander or commander of a large group.
17. Women guards.
18. Office.
19. Person in command of a group.

20. A group which does the preliminary or rough work—similar to the shock troops in the Army.
21. A Dutch girl's name.
22. Superior.
23. Detachable collars usually made of linen.
24. Unwed German mothers (name of honor during the Hitler regime).
25. Name of a street in the city of Haarlem.
26. Hospital.

Chapter 4

27. "Faster, faster!"
28. One of the prisoners appointed to be responsible for keeping order in a group of huts or buildings order in a group of huts or buildings.
29. Camp leader.
30. World leader—God.
31. Camp police.
32. "Go to work!"
33. Serious abdominal disorder caused by malnutrition.
34. Hymns.
35. "Extra food for pregnant women."
36. Aunt Betsie (Beth).
37. Aunt Cornelia (Kees, nickname).

Chapter 5

38. An expression of affection for the House of Orange.
39. City Hall.

PUBLICATIONS
Fort Washington, PA 19034

This book is published by CLC Publications, an outreach of CLC Ministries International. The purpose of CLC is to make evangelical Christian literature available to all nations so that people may come to faith and maturity in the Lord Jesus Christ. We hope this book has been life changing and has enriched your walk with God through the work of the Holy Spirit. If you would like to know more about CLC, we invite you to visit our website:

www.clcusa.org

To know more about the remarkable story of the founding of CLC International we encourage you to read

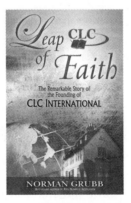

LEAP OF FAITH

Norman Grubb

Paperback
Size 5¹/₄ x 8, Pages 248
ISBN (*trade paper*): 978-0-87508-650-7
ISBN (*e-book*): 978-1-61958-055-8

AMAZING LOVE

Corrie ten Boom

Following her miraculous release from a Nazi concentration camp, Corrie ten Boom refused to give in to the weakness of anger, claiming, "Forgiveness requires more strength than hatred." Sharing incredible stories of encounters with people from all walks of life, Corrie illustrates how a childlike faith in the wisdom and love of God pushes us to forgive the seemingly impossible.

Paperback
Size 5¹/₄ x 8, Pages 122
ISBN (*paperback*): 978-1-61958-288-0
ISBN (*e-book*): 978-1-61958-289-7